MW01254020

PETER

FINDS

POWER

DARYL T SANDERS

This book is a result of a personal Bible study where I reviewed every use of the name of Peter in the Book of Acts. We will look at each of the milestones that Peter was a part of and in which he took action.

It is fascinating how seemingly ill prepared Peter was yet at the same time he fully grasped how to "tap into" the Power of God to take every action he took to start and to build the church of Jesus Christ.

You may contact me at 12dsanders@gmail.com for speaking engagements or questions or discussion

Other books by Daryl T Sanders are:

Peter Finds Life (Peter in the gospels)

Peter Finds Purpose (Peter in the epistles)

God the Father

Finding the Power to Heal

David, Chosen by God

WHY – Questions along life's journey

All Bible references used the King James as found on the web site www.blueletterbible.org. Definitions are from Strong's Concordance

INTRODUCTION

PETER FINDS POWER

We begin our journey through the Book of Acts following the steps of Peter. We will see Peter respond to the infilling of the Holy Spirit and from there preach the first sermon, heal the first sick person, give powerful testimony in court, gain apostolic authority to bring correction to 2 deceivers, he was the first who preached to the gentiles, he water baptized gentiles as well as Jews, he raised the dead, he walked out of prison with the help of an angel – and overall was the first leader and the example to all that would follow him to grow and live and exercise the Power of God available to all believers here on earth.

It is vital that the church stop with the spectator mentality and get moving in the power of God here on earth. As we follow Peter we will see that he learned how to "tap into" what the Holy Spirit was willing to enable Peter to do. As we study his journey ask yourself why he did the things he did on the journey. It happened that believers understood that Peter had found the way to "tap in" to heal the sick, preach to the gentiles, and raise the dead. Discover for yourself how to tap into this same power.

Be prepared to discover how to listen to the Holy Spirit, how to sense the enabling Power coming upon you, how to step out and trust He is with you. Learn how to read the situation and know that it is in you to react and make something happen. It also takes a boldness to step out even before you see where the step will land. It further takes a positive outlook and a trust that God will move upon the situation as you declare His Name to do it.

All too often we are waiting for God to perform the miracle when in fact He is waiting for us to perform the miracle. We are wondering if it is His will and all the time letting Him off the hook with our prayers in doubt. God hates doubt and unbelief. He says that a man who prays in doubt is like a doubled minded man who is unstable in all his ways. If you're in doubt don't pray! Deal with doubt – as in get over it. It is vital to remember that with God all things are possible. With God nothing is too difficult for Him. We often begin allowing ourselves to wonder whether it is his will for this particular moment or person. Jesus said with regular prayer and fasting you will get over your constant doubting application.

CHAPTER ONE
EMPOWERMENT OF THE BELIEVER
PART 1

<u>Acts 1:4-12</u> *And being assembled together with THEM, He commanded them not to depart from Jerusalem, but to wait for the Promise of the Father, "which," HE SAID, "you have heard from Me; for John truly baptized with water, but you shall be baptized with the Holy Spirit not many days from now." Therefore, when they had come together, they asked Him, saying, "Lord, will You at this time restore the kingdom to Israel?"*

And He said to them, "It is not for you to know times or seasons which the Father has put in His own authority. But you shall receive power when the Holy Spirit has come upon you; and you shall be witnesses to Me in Jerusalem, and in all Judea and Samaria, and to the end of the earth." Now when He had spoken these things, while they watched, He was taken up, and a cloud received Him out of their sight.

And while they looked steadfastly toward heaven as He went up, behold, two men stood by them in white apparel, who also said, "Men of Galilee, why do you stand gazing up into heaven? This SAME Jesus, who was taken up from you into heaven, will so come in like manner as you saw Him go into heaven." Then they returned to Jerusalem from the mount called Olivet, which is near Jerusalem, a Sabbath day's journey.

Prior to the above passage it says in *(John 20:21-23 So Jesus said to them again, "Peace to you! As the Father has sent Me, I also send you." And when He had said this, He breathed on THEM, and said to them, "Receive the Holy Spirit. If you forgive the sins of any, they are forgiven them; if you retain the SINS of any, they are retained.")* we see that the disciples were previously born again or saved. That is their spiritual aspect was brought to life by the Holy Spirit and now the Spirit of God could communicate with the spirit in them so that the things of the Kingdom could now be spiritually understood.

But that was not enough – nor should it be enough for us today. Jesus said not only do you need the capacity for spiritual understanding but you need a special infusion of the Power of the Holy Spirit to equip you to do and say the things with authority that the Father wants done on earth.

It is interesting to note that amazingly this "empowerment by the Holy Spirit" has been such a place of division in the church over the last one hundred years. On a worldwide level the Pentecostal or Charismatic movement is actually fueling the evangelism in the world. But in the western cultures of Europe and the USA there is still a contention over the empowerment issue.

It was John the Baptist who first said "I baptize you with water but the One coming after me shall baptize you with the Holy Spirit." John had been "baptized" in the Spirit when he was yet in his mother's womb! He knew that which he spoke of.

In the early days of man on earth God made a "visitation" to earth to see the plans being carried out by mankind under the leadership of a man named Nimrod. They were building a tower to the sky that would provide a worship center for mankind, and they would reach heaven on their own. (See Gen. 11) They also were purposely not "replenishing" the earth but gathering in one spot.

So the Father in His mercy came down and confounded the language of the people. He used language as a means to separate the people into groups so that each group would go and find their own part of earth.

On the day of Pentecost He was using the language that came out of the Baptism of the Holy Spirit to draw people back together so that they could come into unity. The purpose is to take the message of the Savior King to the entire world. So that which disbursed people to inhabit the 4 corners of the world was the same means that God used to gather His people from the 4 corners. When you travel around the world today and you find others that speak your language it is a place of connection and identification. When others speak your language in a foreign country you instantly find camaraderie. When we share our Christian faith in a foreign country that regardless of normal language barriers we find fellowship with other believers that transcends our differences. It is a shame that believers miss out on this fellowship because their dogma prevents them from identifying with one another over the gifting of speaking in tongues. It is God's goal to be used to bring us together and man uses it to keep us from one another.

There are nine gifts of the Holy Spirit and most Christians will agree that seven of them are agreeable and desirable – word of wisdom, word of knowledge, working of miracles (although some teach this is rare if ever), the gift of faith, gifts of healing (also many struggle with), discerning of spirits, and prophecy are all acceptable on some level. But the next two create the most controversy – speaking in tongues and interpretation of tongues.

Perhaps the first seven can generally be more easily understood by the rationale of man. The last two make no sense at all to the natural man. In reality all nine are only truly spiritually discerned and exercised. As with Nimrod (Gen 11) in his time, man continually suffers with the desire to have God on their terms and not on God's terms. We are created in His image after all, and therefore we have a tendency to suffer from the stirrings in our own wicked hearts to have life "my way."

The fact remains that when we journey in life finding out for ourselves how to express the will of God in our own lives that without His Power, or enablement, we will not succeed in doing all that we are called to do. There will be many that could have been Esther's and many that could have been the Daniel's of their day, who missed the opportunity for lack of finding His enabling Power.

Let's consider the whole premise of the journey of Peter's life. His relationship with God was an unfolding and progressive revelation of who God is and what God wanted done in and through Peter's life. Now the question was how would God enable or equip Peter to accomplish or fulfill that call.

But let's be clear here: Jesus said to his disciples who were saved (believing that Jesus died for them and rose again from the dead) and had the breath of the Holy Spirit in them (or the capacity for being able to respond to the Spirit of God) – to go to Jerusalem and wait for the promise of the Father – which was being interpreted that you shall receive Power from on high. Don't miss the progressive nature of all revelation from God. In other words, when I was first "filled or baptized with the Holy Spirit" it was not the end. It was the beginning and would be understood and made more manifest with the exercise thereof.

Many of my contemporaries refuse to use computers. I have heard countless times how they "hate" the computer. What they are really saying is they are afraid of the computer. I began using computers in the later 80's. For me it is quite logical and the evolution of the computer and its growing power to help me accomplish and manage things has been a natural progression.

We started with Internet connections that took forever to get online. The slowness was part of the experience and you just got used to doing things slowly. I started watching TV when I went on the Internet so I had something else to do while I waited for things to happen on the Internet. But magically speed increased seemingly monthly. Available resources multiplied geometrically on the Internet. Email, instant messaging, live phone calls with seeing each other while talking (as I grew up this was called Buck Rogers sci-fi kind of technology), and the myriad of other abilities enabled through the computer has been a great progressive, unfolding experience in education and work. I have come to "love" the computer as I can manage many people in different cities via the Internet and watch over their daily work while in my home office.

This is a great analogy to the working of the Holy Spirit in the life of the believer. As we grow in faith and use of the gifting and applications of the Holy Spirit into our everyday living experience the speed and power and resources multiply in our daily life. It is vital to exercise ourselves in the gifting of the Holy Spirit. The more we learn to rely on Him the more active He becomes in our daily life. Our human tendency is to only "call on Him when we need help." This is foolish, we are talking like God has limits and we want to make sure we don't tax His limits. Or some say I don't want to bother Him! This kind of thinking about God is based on a religious and childish understanding of God.

God is omnipotent – all powerful. God is omniscient – all knowing. God is omnipresent – everywhere at once. We subtract nothing from Him when we interact with Him, His capacity is limitless.

I have heard many say that, "I was baptized in the Spirit when I was saved and I don't 'need' a second experience." My question then is what evidence do you have in your life that reveals the expression of His Power in your life today? I do not seek to minimize the salvation experience or the Power that comes into anyone's life at salvation. But the question in God is what is the current evidence or how does this Power manifest currently in your life?

We are to work out our salvation currently in daily living. Not that we save ourselves but that we reveal our salvation in our relationships with others:

Phil 2:12 *Therefore, my beloved, as you have always obeyed, not as in my presence only, but now much more in my absence, work out your own salvation with fear and trembling; for it is God who works in you both to will and to do for HIS good pleasure.*

There is to be a daily manifestation of our full relationship with God:

<u>Psalm 68:19</u> *Blessed BE the Lord, WHO daily loads us WITH BENEFITS, The God of our salvation! Selah Our God IS the God of salvation;*

Let us not negate nor diminish one another's experience in God, but rather let us encourage one another to find more in God. There is no such thing as one and done in God, but always life and always progressive, and always bearing fruit.

Let me put it bluntly. There is more to God than you or I know. The desire to know Him should be a part of daily life. I want to know Him and understand Him more today than I did yesterday. What is God currently showing you this week that is new to you about Him? Is your testimony about God ten or twenty years old? If it is you are missing out on the "daily benefits" of knowing Him.

If you will read your Bible daily, searching the scriptures to know Him more each day you will find Him. He desires that our relationship with Him be uninterrupted. He doesn't want a weekly relationship or a monthly or an annual relationship.

He desires to give us "our daily bread." That bread is His word and that word is His life and power for the believer.

CHAPTER TWO
EMPOWERMENT OF THE BELIEVER
PART 2

Acts 2:1-8 *When the Day of Pentecost had fully come, they were all with one accord in one place. And suddenly there came a sound from heaven, as of a rushing mighty wind, and it filled the whole house where they were sitting. Then there appeared to them divided tongues, as of fire, and ONE sat upon each of them. And they were all filled with the Holy Spirit and began to speak with other tongues, as the Spirit gave them utterance. And there were dwelling in Jerusalem Jews, devout men, from every nation under heaven. And when this sound occurred, the multitude came together, and were confused, because everyone heard them speak in his own language. Then they were all amazed and marveled, saying to one another, "Look, are not all these who speak Galileans? And how IS IT THAT we hear, each in our own language in which we were born?*

There were as many as five hundred people at the ascension of Jesus, but the Bible says "some doubted." There were only one hundred and twenty people that hung in there for ten days seeking Him in prayer in the upper room. But the one hundred and twenty were in "total agreement" gathered together in that place seeking God with all their hearts and soul. The expression, "when Pentecost was fully come" means they were "swamped" with a sound from heaven. This was no casual sit still, bow your head and be quiet kind of meeting. All heaven broke loose! They were making so much noise that passersby took note. What looked like chaos to the observer was going on so loudly and so long that word started buzzing all around Jerusalem.

If you stop and think about it this must have gone on for hours and hours. Interestingly the predominant manifestation was they were all speaking in tongues. There was excitement in the air to be sure with one hundred and twenty people talking and singing at the top of their lungs. It was a day of unity and power manifested that would set the stage for the evangelism of the world by the church.

I have been in meetings where strangers have heard their own language spoken. I was in a Pastor's prayer meeting where the Holy Spirit came in the midst of the Pastors from all denominations, in a sound from heaven that took us to new places in Christ.

One man, with a musical background came out of the meeting in amazement and said, "Did you hear it, did you hear it? There was an octave sound that is humanly impossible to make!" And there were no instruments in the room, all that was there was a group of seventy men in unity seeking the Lord with all their hearts.

Somewhere along life's way the church began to emphasize the solemnity aspect of gathering together. It is a good thing to be reflective at times before God. It can be good to be in a quiet mode sometimes seeking Him for answers or in an attitude of repentance. But this is not the norm, and God is not looking for quiet contemplative people. It is too easy to focus on one's self in this type of setting, and the object of gathering together is to worship and focus on Him.

One only needs to look at the three major feasts of the Old Testament – orchestrated by God – to get a better understanding of how God expects our gatherings to be. Take for example the Feast of Tabernacles, which took place after the time of harvest. First of all everyone quit work for seven days. They gathered in Jerusalem, and literally sang, danced (as unto the Lord), worshipped, and brought extravagant gifts and offerings to God. It was not a time of revelry like we see at Mardi Gras. It was not a time of drunkenness from too much wine.

It was a time of noisy celebration, giving shouts of joy, and celebrating the goodness of God, thanking Him for all His mercies and provisions in the harvest. After all we enter His gates with thanksgiving and His courts with praise. We have reduced the rule of doing "what is decent and in order," down to quietness and self reflection which is far from how God would have us enter into Fellowship with Him and other believers.

All we need do is look at the Book of Revelation to get insight into what a meeting with God really looks like. Several times there it describes spontaneous worship by the twenty four elders that surround the throne. Now these twenty four people are surely the most outstanding people who have ever lived – in God's eyes. The only thing any of us gather while here on earth are those things which will be added to our crowns in heaven. These elders will take those crowns – the only thing that belongs to them – and throw them at the feet of Jesus, acknowledging Him and expressing that their crowns are only because of Him. They worship Him with all their hearts and all their souls and all their minds. They abandon what we think is decorum and good behavior. Rather they extravagantly throw aside their rankings and positions to give complete honor and glory to God in the loudest and humblest showing possible.

Our problem is we have a tendency to not fully realize what Jesus has done for us. Without Him we are lost and carry a sentence of eternal death on our heads. Unfortunately our focus is on what we want Him yet to do for us, without thanking Him for what He already has done. If someone gave you a dollar for a cup of coffee you might say thanks. If someone paid your rent for a month you might say thanks and give a hug. If someone paid your rent every month your heart would soon begin to bear an obligation of thanksgiving that would need to find more generous expression. The more someone would do for us the more gratitude that our heart should seek to express.

Our problem often is that when others are generous with us, we start thinking somehow we deserved it or they should have done that for us. We especially think this when we feel the obligation to express thanksgiving is too great for us to know how to do it. But the Bible is clear – we will praise Him. Praise Him in the morning, praise in the noon, praise Him in our house, and praise Him in the sanctuary. It is not that He "needs" praise but we need to give expression to our obligation of thanksgiving for all He has done for us. He has saved us from eternal damnation, He has saved us from eternal separation from Him, and He has saved us from an eternal existence in the flames of fire.

The empowerment of the Holy Spirit is not a quiet thing. When you know that you know that the Holy Spirit has been unleashed upon you and you are now equipped to tap into that Power as necessary to carry out the will of God in your life it is exciting.

Some misinterpret the excitement of such a meeting as all emotionalisms and a group getting carried away. But emotionalism is not the driving force. Truth of what He has done for us and how He has provided for us is the driving force that is released emotionally, physically, and spiritually.

When you know that you know that God has empowered you to connect with Him via His Holy Spirit it is a wonderful revelation, it is exciting and thrilling, and it is cause for expression in dramatic fashion. One thing I have noticed over the years is that children everywhere – white, black, brown, yellow, or red will dance and jump around when they are happy. They yell and scream and laugh out loud. But in most western cultures we tell them to "act right and quit making so much noise." So in fact, we discipline out of our children the normal human response to the joyful happenings in life.

I remember the day I came back to church after a fifteen year absence. Someone in the congregation said Amen – while the Pastor was still preaching!! I remember thinking, "what is wrong with that guy?" And in subsequent weeks thought you'll never catch me doing that! God has a sense of humor – for as I grew in faith and in understanding of the true nature of God, I readily Amen and give praise as I hear and see His truth preached or practiced. He often places before us those things that grate on our nerves to confront us with our own misguided religious thinking that is actually hindering our relationship with Him.

But let us not reduce the Baptism in the Holy Spirit as simply a matter of speaking in tongues. In reality this empowerment experience looses in us an enabling power to operate in all nine gifts of the Holy Spirit.

<u>1 Cor 12:4-11</u> *There are diversities of gifts, but the same Spirit. There are differences of ministries, but the same Lord. And there are diversities of activities, but it is the same God who works all in all. But the manifestation of the Spirit is given to each one for the profit OF ALL: for to one is given the word of wisdom through the Spirit, to another the word of knowledge through the same Spirit, to another faith by the same Spirit, to another gifts of healings by the same Spirit, to another the working of miracles, to another prophecy, to another discerning of spirits, to another DIFFERENT kinds of tongues, to another the interpretation of tongues. But one and the same Spirit works all these things, distributing to each one individually as He wills.*

The Apostle Paul tells the church some twenty years later how these gifts work. The gifts are diverse meaning they work differently in different people and in different situations. They are administered differently meaning they are expressed and function according to the situation and not the same way every time. The gifts in operation look different and act different and can be expressed differently – but in all these differences they are all from the same God.

The beauty of this empowering relationship we have with God through our faith in Jesus Christ and by the power of the Holy Spirit enable us to do whatever God wants us to do in any and every situation. We can walk fearlessly and openly and trustingly in any situation we find ourselves in knowing that God is with us and will enable us to face it all. He even says take no thought what you will say for the Holy Spirit will speak through you in those times you are on the stand.

The Church of Jesus Christ cannot run on the logic of men. It cannot run on wisdom from earth. It requires a heavenly wisdom. It requires a leading of the Holy Spirit. And it requires men and women who will be sensitive to this leading of the Spirit and requires those who will walk in the Spirit.

We see in the Book of Acts before the outpouring of the Holy Spirit Peter stands up and holds a meeting to replace Judas' position. They drew straws to find the replacement for Judas. Granted he was following scripture but it was an administrative meeting. Then in chapter 2 after the outpouring of the Spirit Peter stood up and began preaching to all those who gathered around this "Holy Spirit meeting" and three thousand people got saved. Empowerment brings action and advancement in the Kingdom of God. Empowerment enables the believer to effectively show the power of God to the unbeliever so that he might be saved.

You will note that the Book of Acts is a book of action. It is not a book of meetings establishing the rules of organization and how to get ahead. As the gifts of the Spirit are manifested in the apostles and other workers in the church great fear came on the believers for they saw firsthand that God was at work through men and women. This kind of fear of God working through men is foreign today but it will return to the church in the end of times.

<u>Eph 5:18</u> *And be not drunk with wine, wherein is excess; but be filled with the Spirit;*

Consider this scriptural analogy: when you are drunk with wine you go places you normally would not go, you do things you would not normally do, and you say things you normally would not say! Likewise being filled with the Spirit works the same way but for good!

As we are empowered by God we will go places we would not go on our own, we will do things that we would not normally do, and we will say things that we would not normally say!

You may go to the penthouse or the outhouse with the words to say that will liberate your listeners. You will do things in power to heal the sick and pray for the poor and set the captives free. You will say words of life to people you don't even know.

There comes a joy when your heart knows and understands first hand – "with God, all things are possible!"

DISCUSSION CHAPTER ONE AND TWO– EMPOWERMENT OF THE BELIEVER PART 1 AND 2

1) How would you describe what can take place after salvation?

2) Describe – fully – the prayer meeting in the upper room.

3) Describe the role of the gifts of the Spirit in the life of the believer.

4) If Jesus told the followers prior to His ascension, that they should go and wait in Jerusalem, what are the implications of that to the church today?

5) What qualifications does God require for church workers today?

CHAPTER THREE
PETER PREACHES THE FIRST SERMON

Acts 2:14-41 *But Peter, standing up with the eleven, raised his voice and said to them, "Men of Judea and all who dwell in Jerusalem, let this be known to you, and heed my words. For these are not drunk, as you suppose, since it is only the third hour of the day. But this is what was spoken by the prophet Joel: 'AND IT SHALL COME TO PASS IN THE LAST DAYS, SAYS GOD, THAT I WILL POUR OUT OF MY SPIRIT ON ALL FLESH; YOUR SONS AND YOUR DAUGHTERS SHALL PROPHESY, YOUR YOUNG MEN SHALL SEE VISIONS, YOUR OLD MEN SHALL DREAM DREAMS. AND ON MY MENSERVANTS AND ON MY MAIDSERVANTS I WILL POUR OUT MY SPIRIT IN THOSE DAYS; AND THEY SHALL PROPHESY. I WILL SHOW WONDERS IN HEAVEN ABOVE AND SIGNS IN THE EARTH BENEATH: BLOOD AND FIRE AND VAPOR OF SMOKE. THE SUN SHALL BE TURNED INTO DARKNESS, AND THE MOON INTO BLOOD, BEFORE THE COMING OF THE GREAT AND AWESOME DAY OF THE LORD. AND IT SHALL COME TO PASS THAT WHOEVER CALLS ON THE NAME OF THE LORD SHALL BE SAVED.'*

"Men of Israel, hear these words: Jesus of Nazareth, a Man attested by God to you by miracles, wonders, and signs which God did through Him in your midst, as you yourselves also know— Him, being delivered by the determined purpose and foreknowledge of God, you have taken by lawless hands, have crucified, and put to death; whom God raised up, having loosed the pains of death, because it was not possible that He should be

held by it. For David says concerning Him: 'I FORESAW THE LORD ALWAYS BEFORE MY FACE, FOR HE IS AT MY RIGHT HAND, THAT I MAY NOT BE SHAKEN. THEREFORE MY HEART REJOICED, AND MY TONGUE WAS GLAD; MOREOVER MY FLESH ALSO WILL REST IN HOPE. FOR YOU WILL NOT LEAVE MY SOUL IN HADES, NOR WILL YOU ALLOW YOUR HOLY ONE TO SEE CORRUPTION. YOU HAVE MADE KNOWN TO ME THE WAYS OF LIFE; YOU WILL MAKE ME FULL OF JOY IN YOUR PRESENCE.'

"Men AND brethren, let ME speak freely to you of the patriarch David, that he is both dead and buried, and his tomb is with us to this day. Therefore, being a prophet, and knowing that God had sworn with an oath to him that of the fruit of his body, according to the flesh, He would raise up the Christ to sit on his throne, he, foreseeing this, spoke concerning the resurrection of the Christ, that His soul was not left in Hades, nor did His flesh see corruption. This Jesus God has raised up, of which we are all witnesses. Therefore being exalted to the right hand of God, and having received from the Father the promise of the Holy Spirit, He poured out this which you now see and hear. "For David did not ascend into the heavens, but he says himself:

'THE LORD SAID TO MY LORD, "SIT AT MY RIGHT HAND, TILL I MAKE YOUR ENEMIES YOUR FOOTSTOOL." '

"Therefore let all the house of Israel know assuredly that God has made this Jesus, whom you crucified, both Lord and Christ." Now when they heard THIS, they were cut to the heart,

and said to Peter and the rest of the apostles, "Men and brethren, what shall we do?" Then Peter said to them, "Repent, and let every one of you be baptized in the name of Jesus Christ for the remission of sins; and you shall receive the gift of the Holy Spirit. For the promise is to you and to your children, and to all who are afar off, as many as the Lord our God will call."

And with many other words he testified and exhorted them, saying, "Be saved from this perverse generation." Then those who gladly received his word were baptized; and that day about three thousand souls were added to them.

(The capitalized words were Peter's quotes from memory of the Old Testament)

The entire text is given above for several reasons. One is that Peter, an unlearned man, a man who had not been educated in the schools of the day. He had not had any formal religious training other than evidently that training by his parents and his experience in walking with Jesus for 3 + years. He was after all a common fisherman. But a man filled with the Holy Spirit commands an authority and clarity that comes by faith in the heart of the speaker. Notice also Peter is quoting several different passages of scripture out of the Book of Joel but also a couple of the Psalms. Being able to pull those quotes together into a coherent sermon is certainly proof of the inspirational power of the Holy Spirit.

In addition, let's see how Peter clarifies or Biblically interprets all the seeming chaos that the people gathered had seen. The visitors evidently thought they were witnessing one hundred and twenty people drunk out of their minds. Now let's face it that conjures up a picture of bedlam. Yet it was in fact the conclusion of the bystanders. So this meeting was taking on a louder, jumping around, dancing, cheering, speaking and singing than most of us have been willing to recognize as to what that meeting looked like.

You can read these couple of lines and not think of the dynamics of the meeting and miss the significance of the behavior of the participants in the meeting. Today when such meetings take place the western bystanders accuse the participants of extreme emotionalism. Thinking such emotionalism is surly not spiritual because we should all be under control and rational.

Time after time when man faces the heavenly in the Bible, being under control is the least of what happens to anyone. Always the person standing falls down, starts shaking, feels dirty, and pleads for mercy and other demonstrations of being in a supernatural presence.

So Peter quotes from the book of Joel to establish a Biblical standard to the goings on.

Then Peter goes into an end time scenario pointing out the world as we all know it is going to have its day of ending. He then goes into very important theological waters. He begins to show how the Messiah had to suffer and die. A lesson he himself had learned firsthand. It is profound to see that the hard lessons learned by Peter were in his first sermon. After all Peter recognized that what troubled him troubled all Jewish people.

He ties Jesus into King David who has always been tied to the Messiah. Then he talks of the resurrection of Jesus as the culmination of the victory over sin and death. That did it! The hearers of this first sermon were "pricked in their hearts." This is the convicting power of the Holy Spirit, when people hear words of life they then know they must do something about the evil of their own hearts. Peter lead them into salvation and baptism and three thousand people were brought into the saving knowledge of Christ on that day.

So let's consider the context here: on the day that a group of one hundred and twenty people who believed that Jesus was their Savior were gathered together seeking God with all their hearts, souls, and minds there was an outpouring of the Holy Spirit on them all.

Then crowds gathered to see all the commotion. Then Peter – the man always at the ready to jump in and take over the situation – stood up and seized the moment by preaching how that Jesus was the One that all Jews had been looking for to be the Messiah.

Notice that Peter was certainly being led by the Spirit and shown what to do on the go, else how would he know what to do? There is no biblical precedence for the conversion of a crowd. But Peter put together the requirements needed at the moment from a combination of the teaching of John the Baptist, the teachings of Jesus, and the Old Testament and he voiced what they needed to do – repent of their sins – be baptized in Jesus' name – and receive the Holy Spirit.

What a glorious beginning for the Church of Jesus Christ!

DISCUSSION CHAPTER THREE -
PETER PREACHES THE FIRST SERMON

1) Look up the scriptures quoted by Peter and list them.

2) Notice how simple the message is – create an outline covering this first sermon.

3) What were key proofs that Jesus was who He said He was?

4) Who made Jesus Lord and Christ? What is the significance of that?

CHAPTER FOUR
PETER AND THE FIRST HEALING MINISTRY
OF THE CHURCH

<u>Acts 3:1-16</u> *Now Peter and John went up together to the temple at the hour of prayer, the ninth HOUR. And a certain man lame from his mother's womb was carried, whom they laid daily at the gate of the temple which is called Beautiful, to ask alms from those who entered the temple; who, seeing Peter and John about to go into the temple, asked for alms.*

And fixing his eyes on him, with John, Peter said, "Look at us." So he gave them his attention, expecting to receive something from them. Then Peter said, "Silver and gold I do not have, but what I do have I give you: In the name of Jesus Christ of Nazareth, rise up and walk." And he took him by the right hand and lifted HIM up, and immediately his feet and ankle bones received strength. So he, leaping up, stood and walked and entered the temple with them—walking, leaping, and praising God.

And all the people saw him walking and praising God. Then they knew that it was he who sat begging alms at the Beautiful Gate of the temple; and they were filled with wonder and amazement at what had happened to him. Now as the lame man who was healed held on to Peter and John, all the people ran together to them in the porch which is called Solomon's, greatly amazed.

So when Peter saw IT, he responded to the people: "Men of Israel, why do you marvel at this? Or why look so intently at us, as though by our own power or godliness we had made this man walk? The God of Abraham, Isaac, and Jacob, the God of our fathers, glorified His Servant Jesus, whom you delivered up and denied in the presence of Pilate, when he was determined to let HIM go. But you denied the Holy One and the Just, and asked for a murderer to be granted to you, and killed the Prince of life, whom God raised from the dead, of which we are witnesses.

And His name, through faith in His name, has made this man strong, whom you see and know. Yes, the faith which COMES through Him has given him this perfect soundness in the presence of you all.

Oh the joy that must have filled the heart of Jesus as He watched Peter at work in the Kingdom of God on earth. Peter and John went to the synagogue as they regularly did even after the resurrection. There had not been time yet to come to grips with the conflict of Jesus redefining the Jewish belief system – and the resistance that would come with that. There was a transformation going on from the Old Covenant to the New Covenant. It was going to take years to work out the details and ramifications of this transformation.

When Jesus preached the "Sermon on the Mount," series in Matthew Chapter 5 He defined the changes that would take place and what the New Covenant would look like in terms of attitudes and behavior. It would take time for these to work their way into the systematic teaching of the early church. So every new step taken under the unction of the Holy Spirit was a joy for Jesus to see in his followers.

This lame beggar was a regular stationed ironically at the gate beautiful. Beggars had their regular stations in and around the city. The key to begging is to get the passerby to look into your eyes. Beggars can talk with their eyes to generate sympathy and also discern with their eyes whether they should keep talking to get the passerby to loosen their purse strings for a hand out.

Notice Peter "fastened" his eyes on the beggar. He was not looking for how pathetic the beggar was he was looking for what the Holy Spirit would direct him to do at that moment. He discerned the Power of God to heal this man. This gift of healing and faith to do the super natural filled Peter to overflowing. "Silver and gold have I none but such as I have give I thee! In the Name of Jesus rise up and walk."

There was no doubt in Peter or John's mind that the healing power of God was at work, so they pulled him up and he began leaping and walking and praising God.

The beggar was famous as it was and everyone had seen him everyday begging for years and years. He had been lame all his life so his healing was of epic news to the city. When everyone gathered to applaud Peter and John, Peter quickly revealed and understood his lessons from Jesus well. This healing was not about Peter it was about Jesus. The Kingdom is not about a healer, preacher, or any Spirit filled believer it is about the love and grace and mercy of Jesus in a fallen world.

Peter is making this same power available to all the listeners by helping them identify that the God of Abraham, Isaac, and Jacob, sent Jesus to make this healing power available along with the power to save us from our sins. Peter is emphasizing how the power is made available not to a few but to all believers – a lesson for all of us to learn today. The Name of Jesus and faith in that Name releases the Power to heal and the Power to save.

<u>Phil 2:9-11</u> *Therefore God also has highly exalted Him and given Him the name which is above every name, that at the name of Jesus every knee should bow, of those in heaven, and of those on earth, and of those under the earth, and THAT every tongue should confess that Jesus Christ IS Lord, to the glory of God the Father.*

Peter had a firm grasp on the truth that he was eligible to use the name of Jesus to heal the sick and save the lost. He understood that not only was he eligible but that he was authorized to use that name.

It is an incredible truth that just as I may give my child a credit card with my name on it to use and the pin number that authorizes him to do so, Jesus authorizes us to use the Power of His Name to reach and save and heal that which is lost. Just as I don't give the card to be used for superfluous things, Jesus does not authorize us to use His Name for the silly or for the personal gain of the user.

The Name of Jesus is precious and powerful and the name that every other thing named must bow to. When an American Ambassador located in another country – let's say England, walks into the Prime Minister's office, he is representing at that moment the President of the United States.

When he speaks or negotiates he is speaking or negotiating in the name of the President. He has been authorized to use and speak in that name. He can sign treaties, make deals, give help, or ask for help with the force of the name he represents. The Ambassador's name doesn't really matter, his credentials are what matter. Does he officially represent the President? This is always the first thing an Ambassador does when assigned to any country, is to present his credentials. This then clarifies the authority to speak in the name of the President.

Peter and John healed the beggar – that established the credentials – or the authority to speak in the Name of Jesus. Therefore when they spoke in the Name of Jesus it was done with a force and power that led five thousand people to the saving knowledge of Christ that day.

This is no small truth.

2Cor 5:20 *Now then we are ambassadors for Christ, as though God did beseech you by us: we pray you in Christ's stead, be ye reconciled to God.*

We have a tendency to minimize our role in representing Christ on earth. It is an important role. We have been authorized to speak and act in His name and we should honor that and live up to that authority. How would I feel if I gave a pre-paid credit card to someone and they starved to death and there was $20,000 on that card that had never been used? It would be both sad and ridiculous.

There is an overwhelming temptation to think that God is micro managing the goings on earth. But the reality is He expects us to do the daily running of events. He will participate as we learn to draw upon Him, His Word, and His Spirit. Yes, there is an overall plan; there is a second coming of Christ on the horizon. There is judgment, woes, and poured out vials of suffering and pain coming to earth as prophesied.

But lest we be fooled, there is an authority and an ability to take action that is available to the believer, and for that matter to the Church. When God tried to send Jonah to Nineveh to preach repentance it was for the purpose of giving the people a chance to forestall the judgment through repentance that Nineveh had called down on herself. When Jonah finally got there and walked the city preaching – the entire city, starting with city leaders, responded and fasted and repented. So that through their repentance at Nineveh the inevitable judgment was put off for forty years. The Lord is watching and waiting for the church to step up and impact our communities, our cities, our nations, and our world to forestall the judgments that are coming.

We do have the power to turn the course of our Nation. The key to the release is in the truth;

2 Chron *If my people, which are called by my name, shall humble*
7:14 *themselves, and pray, and seek my face, and turn from their wicked ways; then will I hear from heaven, and will forgive their sin, and will heal their land.*

We can effect change in our own lives, our family, our business, our church, our city, our state, and our nation. We are so self centered though, that to do what it takes to bring about this change will take a lot of people to be delivered from self absorption and start thinking – not outside the box – but outside their own selfish needs and wants.

Let's go back to Peter and the first public healing performed by a disciple in the New Covenant. When did we lose sight of words spoken by Jesus just before His ascension?

<u>Mark 16:17-20</u> *And these signs will follow those who believe: In My name they will cast out demons; they will speak with new tongues; they will take up serpents; and if they drink anything deadly, it will by no means hurt them; they will lay hands on the sick, and they will recover." So then, after the Lord had spoken to them, He was received up into heaven, and sat down at the right hand of God. And they went out and preached everywhere, the Lord working with THEM and confirming the word through the accompanying signs. Amen.*

These are the **last words spoken by Jesus** while still on earth! When you send off a child to college, or on their wedding day, or on your death bed, the last words spoken you can imagine are the final words of encouragement. They are words you want them to never forget. When did we lose sight of the importance of these manifestations in the lives of **ALL BELIEVERS?**

Why then is it so hard to find an individual let alone a church that regularly operates in these gifts of the Holy Spirit? Unfortunately it is because the world view has permeated the church so that rather than church being led by the Spirit we so often are led by the rationale of human thinking. We will find when we go to heaven that we will have left many unopened gifts here on earth.

34 Peter Finds Power

In order for the full power of God to be put to work on earth, God has chosen to work only through His believers. He has gifted us to be able to do whatever we agree to do in his name and by the leading of his Holy Spirit.

DISCUSSION CHAPTER FOUR – PETER AND THE FIRST HEALING MINISTRY OF THE CHURCH

1) What do you think caught Peter's eye at the gate beautiful?

2) Why did Peter think to use the Name of Jesus in administering healing?

3) How do gifts operate in the life of a believer?

4) How does God choose to work on earth?

5) What does it mean to you to be an Ambassador for Christ?

CHAPTER FIVE
PETER AND JOHN ARRESTED!

<u>Acts 4:6-20</u> *And it came to pass, on the next day, that their rulers, elders, and scribes, as well as Annas the high priest, Caiaphas, John, and Alexander, and as many as were of the family of the high priest, were gathered together at Jerusalem. And when they had set them in the midst, they asked, "By what power or by what name have you done this?"*

Then Peter, filled with the Holy Spirit, said to them, "Rulers of the people and elders of Israel: If we this day are judged for a good deed DONE to a helpless man, by what means he has been made well, let it be known to you all, and to all the people of Israel, that by the name of Jesus Christ of Nazareth, whom you crucified, whom God raised from the dead, by Him this man stands here before you whole. This is the 'STONE WHICH WAS REJECTED BY YOU BUILDERS, WHICH HAS BECOME THE CHIEF CORNERSTONE.' Nor is there salvation in any other, for there is no other name under heaven given among men by which we must be saved."

Now when they saw the boldness of Peter and John, and perceived that they were uneducated and untrained men, they marveled. And they realized that they had been with Jesus. And seeing the man who had been healed standing with them, they could say nothing against it. But when they had commanded them to go aside out of the council, they conferred among themselves, saying, "What shall we do to these men? For, indeed, that a notable miracle has been done through them IS evident to all who dwell in Jerusalem, and we cannot deny

IT. But so that it spreads no further among the people, let us severely threaten them, that from now on they speak to no man in this name."

So they called them and commanded them not to speak at all nor teach in the name of Jesus. But Peter and John answered and said to them, "Whether it is right in the sight of God to listen to you more than to God, you judge. For we cannot but speak the things which we have seen and heard." So when they had further threatened them, they let them go, finding no way of punishing them, because of the people, since they all glorified God for what had been done. For the man was over forty years old on whom this miracle of healing had been performed.

It is amazing how swiftly opposition arose against the works of Peter and John. A few thousand people got "saved" and thousands more were talking about it. But the religious leaders of the Jews put a clamp on it and right now. There was a clear chain of command in that day in the synagogues and how things were done was all by approval and controlled from the High Priest on down. This control was being threatened and existing leadership, that did not have a clue as to the dynamics of what was going on, knew they would be left out of the loop unless they stopped it.

Peter and John and the rest were not a part of the hierarchy and would have to be stopped immediately. Notice how the Power of the Holy Spirit through Peter gave him words to speak without preplanning or preparing in any way. The hierarchy could not argue that there had been notable things take place. So their first question was where does your power come from? Wondering if this was from heaven or hell? Although let's face it, if the power was from heaven they knew they were in trouble. The Jewish hierarchy had cut itself off from the possibility of God moving amongst them in any way outside of their control. Dangerous theology that is that handcuffs how God can or cannot move among us.

We can see the evidence in most "denominations," that certain teachings that had significance in one era may not be quite as significant in another era – yet the leaders hold on to the old fearing the loss of their roots. The point we miss is that there are seasons in life as well as in history. For example, there may have been an importance at the time of birthing of a denomination that the cutting of women's hair represented a social issue that needed to be addressed. There was a revelation of significance at the time in the scripture that talks about women's hair and it was embraced as a word from the Lord. In another day, this issue may have lost some of its significance or importance, yet the denomination holds on to "the rule" and forces the issue by making it a condition imposed on those that want to join them in this new day. Now new people might like the worship experience but cannot grasp the "hair rule" so they won't join and it becomes a point of contention.

They will claim that it is honoring their roots in faith. Yet it becomes a stumbling block and keeps other people from joining with them. This is not unlike what Jesus talked about to the Pharisees. To minimize offending anyone here – let me be clear – when the emphasis is on what we are doing on the outside of ourselves, and not on the inside – a matter of the heart – it can easily be subject to change without disgracing our roots.

They complained to Jesus that there was not a proper washing of the disciples prior to eating. Jesus said you put too much emphasis on the outside of the cup and missed the importance that it is the inside that must be clean. Or another time the Pharisee's complained as the disciples ate as they walked through the field on the Sabbath day. Jesus said something like, "Hey (my suggestion) remember when David and his followers ate the Shewbread?" It was not that rules were made to be broken – but that emphasis and context can over ride a rule. When our rules are set for temporary things then they can be temporarily suspended or done away with completely.

When Peter got up before the court in defense and he clearly and boldly proclaimed that the miracle had been done in the power that resides in the name of Jesus. He went on, "yes that Jesus you had crucified only a few months before, had bestowed a power in His followers that enables us to heal the sick in Jesus' Name. And by the way, that Jesus you crucified was now raised from the dead."

It is of most interest to note that the hierarchy observed that these were not men of learning yet their boldness and clarity was astounding to the learned men of the court. Also take special note: ***the Jewish hierarchy did not dispute the resurrection of Jesus.*** Surly they would have – and right here in court – if there were any grounds whatsoever for disputing the fact of the resurrection. Furthermore on this subject – it is clear the hierarchy did not want the argument regarding the resurrection to be discussed – because then it would have been on the record and become a historical document. They could not produce a body – so they wanted no more talk in court about the matter otherwise they would have had to concede there was in fact the resurrection of Jesus.

In their judgment they concluded there was no denying the miraculous had been done so rather than learn where God was in all of this – rather than try to discern how God may have opened new doors to their faith. They held on to the old way and dismissed the new things of God out of hand. They threatened them and let them go.

There is a term called "religious thinking." It is not a Biblical phrase but it is a Biblical concept that religious leaders held the position or belief system that decides the way God does things is the way He has always done things. There is not room in religious thinking for progressive revelation – nothing new was going to happen – religious people have their holidays down pat. They meet every week and do things the same way week after week. They have an order to things, and that is just the way it is. When the extraordinary happens they make an excuse and make sure it doesn't happen that way again.

Religious thinking puts a control on the relationship with God that is contrary to all that we see of God in the world around us. The myriad colors of sunrise and sunsets and the colors and shapes of leaves; the variety in size, shape, and colors of reptiles, fish and land animals; the magnificence of the universe in its vastness and wonder; the diversity of the people on earth in color and disposition and varied cultures; the sounds of music in voice and instruments; the combinations of these things living in harmony at times; the wonder of it all reveals a God the Father who is anything but the repetitive week in week out "do it the same way" kind of God.

He is not only the God of creation, He is the Creative God. In other words, life and growth and change are the things that would more clearly give us insight to God Himself and His ways. I was raised in a church that about two thirds of the service was the same every week. I imagine God was as bored as I was. In fact He warns us about vain (empty) repetitive prayers.

The word – revelation – means unfolding. God is too much for us to grasp. No matter how big He is in your eyes – He is bigger, grander, more loving, and more powerful than you or I can understand. So the way God works is that He reveals to us more of Himself a little bit at a time. The more we know Him the more we will see and understand and grasp Him and His ways of thinking and doing things. That is why we must seek Him daily with an earnest heart.

When Jesus wept over Jerusalem He wept because of their refusal to see the Messiah that came for them, but was refused by them because He came in a way they did not want or expect! God is a wonder, and we cannot put a clamp on how He must answer us. If your prayer life is telling God how to do something – look out, those prayers rarely get answered. When we appeal e.g. to save a loved one – telling Him how to do it is actually pretty ridiculous. How about just asking and believing He will save your lost loved one anyway that it will take to reach and save that one that is lost?

Religious thinking in the days of the early church bound up the people that had limited their faith to traditional expression. I assure you that when Jesus comes back again the sound will be like the sound of one hundred Niagara Falls'; with the voices of the saints praising the Lord with all their heart and soul. Every one of us must open our hearts to change.

In fact, every one of us should seek Him on more levels, mind, body, and spirit. Seeking to find him in every situation life presents. Find new ways to express thanksgiving, it will bring a new joy to your soul.

There is in several segments of the church in our day that claims that speaking in tongues or speaking prophetically are passed. The flimsy interpretation of the verse used to support this claim is yet to apply. The point here is that God is expanding our opportunity to use His gifts. No where do we see a case that God gave one age a gift and then took it back to let the next age of man not have access to that gift. Quite the contrary, God is revealing more and more of Himself and His gifts become more available from generation to generation. There is no example in the Bible where one generation operated in a gift of God or in a revelation of God and then a subsequent generation was not able to do so. Jesus said greater things will you do than I did!

The Book of Revelation can be said it is about the end of time. But there is another way to look at it. It is in fact, an unfolding or revealing of Jesus in all His glory. The world will finally see Him as He really is. Not some common ordinary looking man like He looked when He came the first time – but when He comes again it will be in all glory, power, and honor. He will be revealed as the King of kings, and the Lord of lords. He will be the most fantastic sight ever seen my Mankind. He will be the most impressive Person ever seen or heard about.

It has been a shortcoming of our human condition that we want to resolve things and claim the way we do things is the right way, as in fact, in our minds the only way. One of the joys of world travel is to see how others do the things we do. You will quickly learn as you visit churches from Russia to Africa to China and everywhere in between that there are as many legitimate ways to worship God as there are people. Only the western church is afraid of emotionalism for some strange reason. Emotions should never be the driving force as to why we do what we do. But emotions do not need to be checked at the door either.

The Jewish leadership could not make room for a new move of God and I am sure that was why Jesus chose a group of unlearned men who could grasp with the help of the Holy Spirit the New Covenant and the freedom it was to bring to people of every tribe, tongue and nation.

DISCUSSION CHAPTER FIVE
PETER AND JOHN ARRESTED!

1) Why did the religious leaders have Peter and John arrested?

2) What were they trying to find out about them?

3) How many different passages did Peter reference in his response?

4) Why did the religious leaders not argue about the resurrection of Jesus?

5) How did Peter grasp the privilege of speaking and praying in "the name of Jesus?"

CHAPTER SIX
PETER ESTABLISHES APOSTOLIC AUTHORITY

<u>Acts 5:1-13</u> *But a certain man named Ananias, with Sapphira his wife, sold a possession. And he kept back PART of the proceeds, his wife also being aware OF IT, and brought a certain part and laid IT at the apostles' feet. But Peter said, "Ananias, why has Satan filled your heart to lie to the Holy Spirit and keep back PART of the price of the land for yourself? While it remained, was it not your own? And after it was sold, was it not in your own control? Why have you conceived this thing in your heart? You have not lied to men but to God."*

Then Ananias, hearing these words, fell down and breathed his last. So great fear came upon all those who heard these things. And the young men arose and wrapped him up, carried HIM out, and buried HIM. Now it was about three hours later when his wife came in, not knowing what had happened. And Peter answered her, "Tell me whether you sold the land for so much?" She said, "Yes, for so much."

Then Peter said to her, "How is it that you have agreed together to test the Spirit of the Lord? Look, the feet of those who have buried your husband ARE at the door, and they will carry you out." Then immediately she fell down at his feet and breathed her last. And the young men came in and found her dead, and carrying HER out, buried HER by her husband. So great fear came upon all the church and upon all who heard these things.

And through the hands of the apostles many signs and wonders were done among the people. And they were all with one accord in Solomon's Porch. Yet none of the rest dared join them, but the people esteemed them highly.

Let's review the details of this scripture a little more clearly. When Ananias came in he brought the money that he and his wife agreed to bring. Peter received a "word of knowledge" that Ananias was lying to God. A word of knowledge of course being one of the nine gifts of the Holy Spirit means that Peter had no way of knowing the facts from anyone whether the gift was the total of the sale as Ananias represented or not. But the Holy Spirit rose up in Peter and gave Peter the facts and Peter knew he was lying so he challenged the lie.

This word of knowledge spoken literally pierced the heart of Ananias and what sounds like a heart attack, struck him down and killed him immediately. Let's make a point that Peter did not kill Ananias. He did not curse him either. He asked him why Ananias let the devil fill his heart with this lie to God. Three hours later his wife came in and Peter certainly understood the gravity of the purpose of the Holy Spirit which was to keep the early leadership of the church pure in motive. Peter gave Sapphira the chance to confess. But he could not warn her to tell the truth. This evil motive was in both her and husband's heart and she needed to seek repentance from her own wrong motives before she lied.

Peter then said how is it that you and your husband both decided to test the Holy Spirit? Peter knew that the curse from lying to the Holy Spirit that fell on her husband had fallen also on her, and when he said the men that buried your husband are on their way to bury you – she keeled over and died. ***Rightly so the fear of the Lord fell on the whole church!***

Apostolic Authority came in such a way that life and healing came to people in the early church through the nine gifts of the Holy Spirit as exercised by the Apostles in their speaking the words inspired by the Holy Spirit. People were healed, saved, delivered from demons, set free and brought back to life. In this case their words were so powerful that when Peter said "why did Satan fill your heart to lie?" That these words in and of themselves struck them down. When the Holy Spirit ministers to us and shows us our wrong doing He gives us a sense of conviction that we recognize we need to repent for our wrong doing. When we are hiding and lying and not wanting to do what is right and we are shown wrong doing our own heart will condemn us. This overwhelming self condemnation struck at the very heart of both Ananias and Sapphira and struck them dead.

In all my years around the church and in all the different circles I have had the privilege of working in and with; I have never heard a sermon about the judgment and death of Ananias and Sapphira. There is a clear message here though. Advancement and promotion in the Kingdom of God are not for sale. Let's look at the context of this judgment;

<u>Acts 4:33-37</u> *And with great power the apostles gave witness to the resurrection of the Lord Jesus. And great grace was upon them all. Nor was there anyone among them who lacked; for all who were possessors of lands or houses sold them, and brought the proceeds of the things that were sold, and laid THEM at the apostles' feet; and they distributed to each as anyone had need.*

And Joses, who was also named Barnabas by the apostles (which is translated Son of Encouragement), a Levite of the country of Cyprus, having land, sold IT, and brought the money and laid IT at the apostles' feet.

There was a great pouring out of surrender by all involved in the early church. There would be travel costs; food costs, shelter costs and all the early workers left their vocations to serve God. So those that had any valuables sold them and threw the money in the "pot" to be distributed as needed.

A man named Joses (Barnabas) was one such man who sold out, and he was appointed to apostleship. This same Barnabas later became a friend and initial mentor to Saul of Taurus or the Apostle Paul. It was clear that his gift was not given out of greed and desire for a position. His gift was given to advance the Kingdom of God. Evidently Ananias and Sapphira took note and conspired in their thinking that if they sold their home and threw in the money they could also become apostles.

There was a catch in their plan. They mutually agreed to hold back a portion – to maybe hedge their bet – to keep something for themselves from the proceeds of the sale-just in case it did not all work out. They evidently did not want to put all their trust for their finances into the leadership of the early church. Oddly, they came before Peter at separate times. Each had their own audience and neither could blame the other. They were each asked when they presented the offering – did you sell for such and such. They each answered yes. They were each struck down dead.

The judgment of God came not because they kept a portion for themselves. There was not then nor is there now a law you must sell your house and possessions and give it all to the church. The judgment came because they lied about it. Their motives were now certain in that what they gave- was lying for purpose of promotion.

Great fear came on everyone because of the death of these two. There is an expression that says you can't "play church." It was particularly crucial in the early days of the church for the Holy Spirit to keep close watch on wrong motives. Evidently leadership authority carries a separate kind of weight of responsibility. There are examples throughout church history of those that abused or misused their authority in the church and suffered consequences including death or misery.

One of our themes in the life journey of Peter in scriptures has been to see how our role is to make ourselves eligible for His use. To what degree or how we are to be used is to be left to Him. Our eligibility is based on purity and a heart after God's own heart. He is looking at the motives of the heart – this is what moves Him to use us.

Just because we cannot count the consequences of sudden death attributable to such an act as clearly today rest assured it still happens. Many "fallen" leaders and many "fallen" in the pew have suffered similar consequences. We have been promised that judgment will begin in the House of God.

We don't very often see the consequences of lying, cheating, or manipulating to get ahead played out so abruptly as with these two. The church is much more stable today and can handle the misuses and abuses suffered at the hands of men. But rest assured – let the fear of the Lord come upon all who read this – the Lord is not slack with His judgments – patient yes, slack no.

Over the history of the church we have seen small groups rise up from time to time with this revelation to sell all and live together in a "community of believers." Just because it was done in the early church does not mean it "must be done today." Likewise, there is a permission to do it if the community so desires. Historically, it has been found that such groups have a tendency to be trapped by the whims of a small group of leaders. One other trap is that they have a tendency to cloister themselves off, which is contrary to the Biblical charge to go out to all the world making disciples.

DISCUSSION CHAPTER SIX
PETER ESTABLISHES APOSTOLIC AUTHORITY

1) Create a list of reasons of why you think Ananias and Sapphira conspired to test the Holy Spirit.

2) Wasn't Peter harsh toward Ananias? If so why? If not why?

3) Why do you think we don't see more people drop over dead today for wrong motives in dealing in the church?

4) What was the general reaction to people outside the church who heard of these deaths?

5) What happened to the expansion plans of the church when word got out that they died?

CHAPTER SEVEN
PETER'S SHADOW HEALS!!

Acts 5:14-16 *And believers were increasingly added to the Lord, multitudes of both men and women, so that they brought the sick out into the streets and laid THEM on beds and couches, that at least the* **shadow of Peter** *passing by might fall on some of them. Also a multitude gathered from the surrounding cities to Jerusalem, bringing sick people and those who were tormented by unclean spirits, and they were all healed.*

Shadow **a)** shade caused by the interception of light **b)** an image cast by an object and representing the form of that object

I wonder how many seminaries in the world are advocating (and training?) to our future church leaders how to gather the power of heaven within themselves so that this power can even translate to their shadow so that the sick are healed while walking in that shadow?

Isn't the definition of shadow interesting? "Shade caused by the interception of light." Who is the light of the world? Yes it is Jesus. And we can intercept that light and apply the power of that light to heal the sick! Also, notice the second definition says the shadow represents the form or person who casts it. This means that the anointing or the qualities that the person has can have an effect and express the Power of God that resides in that person. So their shadow then gives off the same power that the person has.

Now this kind of thinking flies in the face of conventional and "rational" thinking. But maybe that is the point. The truth of God does not require rational thinking. The things of God often don't make sense before the fact. But somehow after the fact they are quite logical. Consider the time Jesus healed the blind man:

<u>John 9:1-7</u> *Now as JESUS passed by, He saw a man who was blind from birth. And His disciples asked Him, saying, "Rabbi, who sinned, this man or his parents, that he was born blind?"*

Jesus answered, "Neither this man nor his parents sinned, but that the works of God should be revealed in him. I must work the works of Him who sent Me while it is day; THE night is coming when no one can work. As long as I am in the world, I am the light of the world."

When He had said these things, He spat on the ground and made clay with the saliva; and He anointed the eyes of the blind man with the clay. And He said to him, "Go, wash in the pool of Siloam" (which is translated, Sent). So he went and washed, and came back seeing

The blind man was born that way. Isn't it probable that he had no eye balls to see? Are we not formed out of the dust of the ground? Was Jesus "merely" performing a creative miracle and taking the dust of the ground and adding His DNA and creating two new eyeballs so the man could see. Wasn't this how the entire person of Adam was created? So it was nothing new!

So, spitting on the ground and applying the wet dust to the eye sockets makes no rational sense before it is done. But after the Holy Spirit inspires and empowers Jesus to perform this miracle our rational minds catch up after the fact and accept what has been done – for now the man can see! We must move beyond the skeptical and doubtful thinking of this age. We must not become prisoner in our spiritual lives to the current conventional wisdom. God is greater than we can think or imagine. God will work in us and through us according to the measure of our faith as we move forward in agreement with Him.

Peter was the man of all the men that walked with Jesus that best understood that what Jesus represented here on earth so too could Peter also represent. Jesus represented all that is good. He is the light of the world. What does that mean? Before Jesus came to the earth the world was in gross darkness. Few could comprehend the spiritual side of life. But when Jesus came and died for us He opened our eyes to enable us to comprehend the heavenly. The light of Jesus opened our eyes to enable us to see GOD!

I am quite sure that most of us have dismissed this account of a shadow healing the sick as some aberration of faith. Surly, that only could have happened for some odd reason within a few months or a couple of years after the day of Pentecost. As if the anointing would wear out or something. This is where human reasoning fails. When we stop to break it down in detail and begin to question how and why did this happen, then we realize it is our doubts that make no sense.

No where does the scripture declare that this method of healing would stop. We have become so filled with doubt and unbelief that we are willing to let the world explain away all the blessings of the Kingdom of God that is ours while we are still on this earth. We have let the thief steal from us how to explore and discover what is ours.

Peter was the man who best serves us as the example who discovered and used the power of God in his everyday life. He discovered that God would inspire – which means breathe into the heart of Peter – when the Power of the Holy Spirit was to be released to do the work of the Kingdom of God here on earth. Remember the prayer – "thy Kingdom come thy will be done, on earth as it is in heaven." This is our mandate. We are to implement the ways of God here on the earth.

We have lost sight of this fact. We have somehow come to think that our relationship with Jesus is to be characterized by our church attendance only. We have lost sight (!) of the fact that we are to likewise demonstrate the power of God that will manifest in healing the sick and otherwise impacting for good the lives of those around us. Did He not promise that He would be with us confirming the work of our hands with signs and wonders? The question to the church then is where are these signs and wonders?

How did Peter heal the sick via his shadow? First of all let's look at his track record here even as early as Acts 5. He already had stood up and preached a comprehensive life changing sermon that impacted three thousand people to repent and give their lives to Jesus. How did he do that? He stood up and without further study just began speaking. Lo and behold the Holy Spirit gave him utterance. In other words he just started talking and the Holy Spirit began to give him the next words to say.

Consider the scripture:

John14:26 *But the Comforter, which is the Holy Ghost, whom the Father will send in my name, he shall teach you all things, and bring all things to your remembrance, whatsoever I have said unto you.*

Look at what Jesus said about His own speech in **John 14:10**... *"The words that I speak unto you I speak not of myself: but the Father that dwelleth in me,"*

But even more than these let's go back to what Jesus taught and scholars forgot or never learned how to implement or apply in their own lives

Mark 13:11 *But when they shall lead [you], and deliver you up, take no thought beforehand what ye shall speak, neither do ye premeditate: but whatsoever shall be given you in that hour, that speak ye: for it is not ye that speak, but the Holy Ghost.*

Consider these words "whatsoever shall be given you...that speak" This should excite the heart of every believer. This is how God works. He is looking for the willing. He is looking for agreement. He is looking for those available. Then He enables by giving whatever is needed for the situation.

After being around the church quite closely for around forty years now, and in full time ministry for thirteen of those years, the number one shortcoming that I have observed in the church is the availability of the people to do the work of the Kingdom of God on this earth. Everywhere I have gone I have heard excuses like as soon as I pay this off or that off, when the kids get out of school, or I am not smart enough, or on and on and on a never ending list of reasons.

It is clear and obvious that Jesus did not wait on Peter and the disciples to get themselves ready before He could send them to start the church! He took them as they were. They were available and willing – that is all God needs! In fact, if we were to sit down and pretend there was no church and we are a group gathered to plan the birth of the church would we have used a small group of unlearned men to do so? Furthermore, would we have just let them go and told them to go to Jerusalem and pray and wait for further instructions?

If you stop and think about it God's ways are certainly higher than our ways. I can't imagine trying to build a whole new institution and bring forth a whole new way of life through such a group as Jesus started the church with. It should show us that any of us any where can do anything that He calls us to do and that He enables us to do.

DISCUSSION CHAPTER SEVEN
PETER'S SHADOW HEALS

1) What is a shadow?

2) How could a shadow heal somebody?

3) How does logic and rational thinking hinder the things of God?

4) How do we as believers come to more fully walk in the Power of God?

5) How can we better work with the Holy Spirit?

CHAPTER EIGHT
PETER AND JOHN ARRESTED
A SECOND TIME

<u>Acts 5:24-42</u> *Now when the high priest, the captain of the temple, and the chief priests heard these things, they wondered what the outcome would be. So one came and told them, saying, "Look, the men whom you put in prison are standing in the temple and teaching the people!"*

Then the captain went with the officers and brought them without violence, for they feared the people, lest they should be stoned. And when they had brought them, they set THEM before the council. And the high priest asked them, saying, "Did we not strictly command you not to teach in this name? And look, you have filled Jerusalem with your doctrine, and intend to bring this Man's blood on us!"

But Peter and the OTHER apostles answered and said: "We ought to obey God rather than men. The God of our fathers raised up Jesus whom you murdered by hanging on a tree. Him God has exalted to His right hand TO BE Prince and Savior, to give repentance to Israel and forgiveness of sins. And we are His witnesses to these things, and SO also IS the Holy Spirit whom God has given to those who obey Him."

When they heard THIS, they were furious and plotted to kill them. Then one in the council stood up, a Pharisee named Gamaliel, a teacher of the law held in respect by all the people, and commanded them to put the apostles outside for a little while. And he said to them: "Men of Israel, take heed to yourselves what you intend to do regarding these men. For some time ago Theudas rose up, claiming to be somebody. A number of men, about four hundred, joined him. He was slain, and all who obeyed him were scattered and came to nothing. After this man, Judas of Galilee rose up in the days of the census, and drew away many people after him. He also perished, and all who obeyed him were dispersed. And now I say to you, keep away from these men and let them alone; for if this plan or this work is of men, it will come to nothing; but if it is of God, you cannot overthrow it—lest you even be found to fight against God."

And they agreed with him, and when they had called for the apostles and beaten THEM, they commanded that they should not speak in the name of Jesus, and let them go. So they departed from the presence of the council, rejoicing that they were counted worthy to suffer shame for His name. And daily in the temple, and in every house, they did not cease teaching and preaching Jesus AS the Christ.

Peter leads the way again. He became more confident in God which can be seen in the degree of his arguments before the court. There is a principle of growth in the Power of the Holy Spirit that we can witness as we consider how quickly Peter expressed a new found authority and boldness. This principle of growth seems to manifest the more we operate in and exercise His Gifts in our lives. When we call upon the words of scripture – therefore we must read them daily! – and flow in the spirit letting our selves be released in trusting His empowerment as we speak and move forward, we will all grow in the use of the gifting of God that is in all of us.

This is important for all of us. We are representatives of Jesus Christ here on earth. He has empowered us to operate in the gifts of the Spirit. In all human disciplines there are basics to know about and practice in everyday living. While in high school I got A's in geometry and trigonometry. 30 years later I looked at a geometry book and it was "Greek to me!" I could no more work out a basic problem than to speak Chinese. Why? Because I had not practiced what I at one time learned. I forgot the rules or laws of geometry, and other than a few symbols I could no longer "think" in geometric terms.

The average Christian does not read their Bible more than once per month! There is a discipline required that somehow has gotten lost in the general life of the church. We don't think generally in Kingdom kind of thinking. We don't pray other than for our needs. We don't praise unless we happen to go to a church that praises – and then we only praise once a week in church if that. We don't operate in the gifts of the Holy Spirit more than once or twice per year.

The result of the lack of discipline and practice of Kingdom living dries up our faith. We hang on to salvation but that is about the extent of our faith. Most Christians wallow in doubt and unbelief. These developed traits hinder the working of the Holy Spirit and hinder Kingdom living. Therefore when called to give a reason for our faith, most Christians stumble around without a convincing argument.

Back to Peter, he faces those in church authority with an argument that while bold, was also confrontive in insinuating that they had actually killed Jesus. You see the conundrum of the religious leaders. If they recognize Power in the Name of Jesus, they had no way to be exonerated for killing Him. They would lose their authority – which they held higher than trying to get on this bandwagon of new found excitement in God permeating the city.

At the same time Peter was laying down a new behavior for believers. It is more important to obey God than to obey any man. This was new teaching for the Jew. The Jewish believer up until this time was always under the control of the leadership from the High Priest on down. What they said went. The Priest was the one who went to God on behalf of the people. Since the days of Moses it was that the people did not go directly to God but trusted the office of the Priest to represent them and their needs to God. They likewise depended on the prophet to bring the Word of the Lord to them.

The Old Covenant was based on human representation officially interceding between God and man. Jesus did away with that separation. The veil was rent. In other words, everyone was now eligible to go to God on their own. Because of the sacrificial Blood of Jesus the way was paved for each person to go to God to repent and pray directly as well as receive directly from God the words of life

In addition, during this court appearance Peter introduces to the hierarchy the Person of the Holy Spirit. They of course ignored such reference because the last thing they wanted to get involved with was a theological discussion with these unlearned fishermen – and lose.

Gamaliel, a man evidently seeking to better understand just exactly what was going on, came up with a compromise that appealed to the religious leaders who governed as if running a political kingdom rather than a spiritual kingdom. His appeal was if God is in this we can't stop it, if God is not in it, it will go away.

This brought relief and release to the early church for many days. But it is a sad day when the church follows the "political kingdom" rules of thinking and engagement. I have found it necessary when I read accounts such as the above, that I ask God how much "political" thinking has crept into my way of looking at things. It is quite clear that the longer we are in a denomination or local church body, the more likely we are to have our own idiosyncrasies. We easily become convinced that the way we do things is the right way – or worse the only way, and we run the risk of missing the new things and ways God may want to move in our midst.

You will notice that when Peter begins to talk about repentance and forgiveness of sins that a great condemnation fell upon the religious leaders. It was taken as a clear attack on the religious leadership of Israel and caused a reaction of hatefulness and murder in the hearts of those leaders.

Now the difference between condemnation and conviction is important to understand. In Christ, when we hear words of correction or judgment (conviction) we will have a response that we must repent for that which is spoken to us. When we are not in Christ and such words come (condemnation) we will have a response to "fight." We become defensive, argumentative, and will often lash out against the messenger. They can be the same words spoken to different people.

We need to understand how the religious leaders were thinking and responding in the days of the early church for those same days are upon us again. The church fights religious thinking from within more than the demonic inspired from without. We are inundated with conventional wisdom that avoids judgments against one another and criticisms against one another. Therefore the church becomes a harmless social entity that not only has little impact in the culture it has little impact within its own 4 walls.

In the end times we will see men of God exercise authority over every level of nature from healing to raising the dead to stopping the rain. At the same time we will see lying wonders done under the inspiration of the devil. It will take discernment to distinguish the difference. It will take a heart after God to be open to the remarkable changes in the manifestations of the Holy Spirit. We can expect confusion and fear to run rampant over the change. We will see many believers fall away. Likewise we will see many unbelievers come to the faith.

We will see religious leaders jump to condemn both the good and the bad. We will see criticisms and judgments run rampant. We "must needs" be prepared and flexible. It is vital everywhere that Christians get into their Bibles daily. We must pray daily for "others" as well as for ourselves. We must pray for the power to witness the goodness of God in our lives. We must praise him daily and pray in the Holy Spirit. The early church prayed for boldness – which means – "all out-spokeness." Of course, it is hard to do when we are doing the same things that the people we are witnessing to are doing.

There is a great lukewarmness upon the church today.

Rev. 3:14-17 *"And to the angel of the church of the Laodiceans write, 'These things says the Amen, the Faithful and True Witness, the Beginning of the creation of God: "I know your works, that you are neither cold nor hot. I could wish you were cold or hot. So then, because you are lukewarm, and neither cold nor hot, I will vomit you out of My mouth. Because you say, 'I am rich, have become wealthy, and have need of nothing'— and do not know that you are wretched, miserable, poor, blind, and naked—*

In a time of great economic and political uncertainty you would think that the church would be in a time of great growth as more and more people turned to the Lord for answers. But as of this time (early 2010) this is not happening. With foreclosures the highest in history with unemployment over 10%, everyone seems to just be trudging forward without seeking God.

These are clear signs of a church that is lukewarm. We are not on fire enough to draw those in need to our meetings. What should be the attitude of the church at this time? We must live in a repentive attitude. We must humble ourselves, fast, and pray for our friends and family and neighbors. It is a time to seek God with all our hearts and mind and soul.

DISCUSSION CHAPTER EIGHT –
PETER AND JOHN ARRESTED A SECOND TIME

1) Describe Peter's progressive operation in the Holy Spirit from the day of Pentecost until this second arrest.

2) Describe what it takes on the part of a believer to "grow in the Holy Spirit."

3) What problems did the Jewish hierarchy face with the confrontation from Peter

4) What are the biggest issues facing a believer that hinders his progression in the faith?

CHAPTER NINE
PETER "SENT"

Acts 8:4-8 *Therefore those who were scattered went everywhere preaching the word. Then Philip went down to the city of Samaria and preached Christ to them. And the multitudes with one accord heeded the things spoken by Philip, hearing and seeing the miracles which he did. For unclean spirits, crying with a loud voice, came out of many who were possessed; and many who were paralyzed and lame were healed. And there was great joy in that city.*

Acts 8:12 *But when they believed Philip as he preached the things concerning the kingdom of God and the name of Jesus Christ, both men and women were baptized.*

Acts 8:14-17 *Now when the apostles who were at Jerusalem heard that Samaria had received the word of God, they sent Peter and John to them, who, when they had come down, prayed for them that they might receive the Holy Spirit. For as yet He had fallen upon none of them. They had only been baptized in the name of the Lord Jesus. Then they laid hands on them, and they received the Holy Spirit.*

Let's get the context and dynamics of this account. I have skipped and selected certain verses only in order to keep on point for purposes of this chapter. Saul of Tarsus was making havoc of the church. So the church leaders (Apostles) sent preachers everywhere away from Jerusalem to preach the Good News of Jesus Christ. They sent Philip to Samaria to preach. Philip was one of the seven deacons selected to serve the church in Jerusalem. Philip went to Samaria and took the city by storm. He preached in great power and he healed the sick and cast out demons.

Strangely yet there was something missing. The new converts all got baptized in water and believed on Jesus Christ as their Savior. But there was still something missing. The Apostles back in Jerusalem heard of the great success of Philip and yet knew something was missing, so they sent Peter and John to tend to the issue.

This is an important understanding of the ways of God in the process of salvation. This account shows us there is a twofold revelation of the Holy Spirit. When these believers were "saved" they received the Holy Spirit – which awakened the spirit within them. Their human spirit was able to comprehend from the Holy Spirit that Jesus was truly their Savior and that they were saved.

Therefore, their own spirit is able to comprehend spiritual things in the spiritual dimension of the Kingdom of God while on earth. It is important to realize that we are more than physical beings. It was the "spirit" in man that died in the Garden of Eden via original sin. So at the time of faith in Christ and repentance for sins we become born again.

Now when we receive His Spirit at the time of salvation we are then enabled to understand spiritual things. So it is an enablement that happens within all of us who believe. Of course just because we are "able" doesn't mean we do. We must exercise this enabling power and develop it. This happens best through regularly and diligently reading our Bible and asking the Holy Spirit to guide us into all truth.

These new believers in Samaria were properly water baptized, which became the way for believers to identify with the death and resurrection of Jesus. It is a method for coming into agreement with God. A Biblical word to describe this agreement is called a covenant. A covenant involves more than simply saying ok to a plan. It is more than making a deal – you do this and I'll do that.

It is a blood covenant that Jesus established by His death – shedding His blood – and His resurrection – that is proof that His blood was sufficient payment for the sins of believers. We enter the covenant relationship when we believe that what Jesus did was for us personally as well as for others.

His Holy Spirit given at salvation is a down payment of more to come. One of the original deacons of the church named Phillip went down to Samaria and preached in the Power of the Holy Ghost, healing the sick, and leading many into salvation and water baptism. But what was missing in their experience was that the new believers had not been "baptized" into the Holy Spirit with evidence of speaking in tongues or any of the other gifts of the Holy Spirit.

It is curious that Phillip did not or could not get the new believers baptized into the Holy Spirit. The report that came back to Jerusalem was that the new believers did not experience this baptism. They were of course water baptized demonstrating that they believed that Jesus died and rose again to save them from their sins. It is not good theology to read too much into what is not said about things in the scripture. So let's take it for what it does say.

Under the ministry of Phillip the new believers in Samaria were not baptized in the Holy Spirit. The leadership of the early church sent Peter and John to Samaria to correct this short coming. They evidently thought it was vital to "complete" the relationship of these new believers with Christ. So Peter and John were sent to pray for and "lay hands on the new believers" so they might receive the Baptism of the Holy Spirit. So they did just that, they called a meeting or series of meetings and they reached all these new believers and that which was missing came to them.

There was evidence that they received this Baptism because it was apparent to all around and especially to one called Simon who previously had been a sorcerer. Baptism in the Holy Spirit is with evidence of Power coming upon the believer. The evidential power could come in many forms but the most common is with speaking in tongues. Simon, the former sorcerer, was so intrigued by the power that happened upon impartation from Peter and John laying hands on the new believers that he offered to buy the "trick or the secret" to how to exercise this power.

When people are baptized in the Holy Spirit there is a demonstrated change in behavior. Things take place that "prove" to those around that there has been a "visitation" in the life of the believer. Weeping, crying tears of joy, dancing, shaking, speaking in tongues, prophesying, words of wisdom and knowledge, prayers of healing, are all examples of the kinds of things that can take place. Jesus promised that the Holy

Spirit would "come upon" them. One translation even indicates that "you will be clothed with Power from on high." It is an encounter with heaven in the life of each believer. It is supernatural in scope and grand enough to elicit physical, emotional, and psychological responses from those so apprehended.

Why does this dimension of the Holy Spirit come upon believers? To enable all believers everywhere to give power in their witness to the unsaved world they live in. Evidently the Father had always planned that "Another like Him" would walk alongside each and every believer after the resurrection of Jesus. Each believer would then give more than words of life to others, but would in fact be empowered to give life itself to the spirit of others just as they had received. Christianity is not merely words or principles but actually power and life itself.

It should also be noted that via the laying on of hands was the means used to convey this empowerment. There may be those that discount this method, but don't. There has been the power of impartation via the laying on of hands throughout the Bible. Jacob laid hands on the heads of Joseph's two sons to impart prophetic words of destiny for each. The high priest laid hands on the sacrificial lamb to impart the sins of the congregation. Impartation is a means to be used in the Kingdom of God in the church. The Apostle Paul later laid hands on Timothy for imparting gifts, especially the gift of faith.

Before we leave this event in the life of Peter let us consider the ramifications that the Apostles in Jerusalem "sent Peter and John." The actual definition of the word Apostle means to "be sent." When someone is sent it conveys the thought that the person is not there on their own or because it "seemed like a good idea." Rather it conveys more the thought that there is agreement from the senders that those sent are on a mission that others believe in as well as they do. The significance of this is that when 2 or 3 agree on earth as touching anything it shall be done. So the "sending" of someone means that they are coming with the authority that resides in the power of agreement on earth.

Matt 18:18-20 *Assuredly, I say to you, whatever you bind on earth will be bound in heaven, and whatever you loose on earth will be loosed in heaven.*

"Again I say to you that if two of you agree on earth concerning anything that they ask, it will be done for them by My Father in heaven. For where two or three are gathered together in My name, I am there in the midst of them."

The sending of ministers is a very weighty gifting to be understood in the western church today. First of all, most of us in the west take pride in our right to our own opinion. We even sometimes say, "Well let me put my two cents in on this question." The problem in the local church is that when we have so many opinions we never operate in the "principle of agreement." We wonder why the church seems so impotent in this day and age – and it is impotent because people claim the right to their own opinions.

Look at what Paul said to the Corinthian church:

1 Cor 1:10 *Now I plead with you, brethren, by the name of our Lord Jesus Christ, that you all speak the same thing, and that*

there be no divisions among you, but that you be perfectly joined together in the same mind and in the same judgment.

Oh, that the church would learn how to walk in the power of the "same mind."

This is Kingdom thinking. We miss the principle of how authority works to establish what should be agreed upon – so that then our prayers may be answered. Our agreement on earth moves heaven to action. It should be clear that Peter and the other Apostles became the hands, feet, voice, and power of Jesus here on earth. If you stop and consider that under the Old Covenant God the Father chose to express Himself through the Jewish Nation. Under the Old the Father showed the world how He thinks and acts and relates with people through the Jews.

Now under the New Testament the Father wants to express Himself through the church of Jesus Christ. So we are not here on earth to create our own agenda. We are not here to accomplish our own will. This life on earth in the church is not about us. It is about Him and about His will.

Mark 16:14-18 *Later He appeared to the eleven as they sat at the table; and He rebuked their unbelief and hardness of heart, because they did not believe those who had seen Him after He had risen. And He said to them, "Go into all the world and preach the gospel to every creature. He who believes and is baptized will be saved; but he who does not believe will be condemned. And these signs will follow those who believe: In My name they will cast out demons; they will speak with new tongues; they will take up serpents; and if they drink anything deadly, it will by no means hurt them; they will lay hands on the sick, and they will recover."*

Jesus spoke to the eleven disciples in verses 14 and 15, and then He included us and spoke to us in verses 17 and 18. We have clear direction. And again Matthew says it this way:

<u>Matt 28:18-20</u> *And Jesus came and spoke to them, saying, "All authority has been given to Me in heaven and on earth. Go therefore and make disciples of all the nations, baptizing them in the name of the Father and of the Son and of the Holy Spirit, teaching them to observe all things that I have commanded you; and lo, I am with you always, EVEN to the end of the age."*

God the Father chose Jesus to represent the Godhead bodily here on earth. Jesus came and lived in perfection, died for our sins, and rose again for our salvation. He then sent forth the Holy Spirit to abide in the hearts of all believers. He then expects us to cover the earth with His power working within the physical bodies of all believers to express Him and His goodness and power on earth in day to day circumstances. We cannot afford the damage that our own opinions can do in hindering agreement in the local body of believers. We must trust that the people who have been sent to minister among us in our local body are heaven sent and we must find agreement by giving up our own preferences and desires and seek agreement whenever possible. When we come to agreement in our tithing and our willingness to follow those sent (even when we are tempted to disagree) the church will flow in the fullness of the glory and power of God to reach and save those who are lost.

So let's back up a moment here. The early church worked in this fashion. The eleven disciples added a replacement for Judas giving them twelve men whose identity changed from disciples to Apostles. This identity was given to several others in the book of Acts and Romans 16:7. An apostle is "one who is sent." The authority then comes from the one doing the sending. Ultimately the sender is Jesus.

Romans 1:1, 2 *Paul, a bondservant of Jesus Christ, called TO BE an apostle, separated to the gospel of God which He promised before through His prophets in the Holy Scriptures,*

So there is spiritual authority – not a hierarchy – but a functioning of gifting that works through men and women of God for the purposes of maturing believers and helping them grow in the faith to more adequately serve Christ here on earth.

Eph 4:11-13 *And He Himself gave some TO BE apostles, some prophets, some evangelists, and some pastors and teachers, for the equipping of the saints for the work of ministry, for the edifying of the body of Christ, till we all come to the unity of the faith and of the knowledge of the Son of God, to a perfect man, to the measure of the stature of the fullness of Christ;*

Thus we see that Jesus works through the gifting He places in men and women to enable the church to function and succeed in the goal of making disciples in all the nations of the world. It is up to the "gifted one" to grow and function in his or her gifting to maximize usefulness while here on earth. So our connection is directly to Jesus and is verifiable as we walk in the power of the Holy Spirit. That being said then our church cannot be at the mercy of the opinions of the general congregation. There should be a fear in our hearts and carefulness in our words when moving and living in the church community.

How can this ever happen in a practical step by step way? First of all I have not seen it yet! But what seems obvious to me is that all of our opinions need to be checked at the door of the sanctuary. We need to come in free from our own prejudices and our own way of looking and seeing things. Each one must seek the mind of Christ; here is what the Apostle Paul wrote to the Romans:

<u>Rom 15:6, 7</u> *that you may with one mind AND one mouth glorify the God and Father of our Lord Jesus Christ. Therefore receive one another, just as Christ also received us, to the glory of God.*

Now imagine with me what would have to happen in each of our hearts that we would have one mind? In order for the group to have one mind we would first need to give up our claim to having our own mind on the matter of church! Then we would have to "receive" one another, and the key here is that we receive one another just as we are.

How is this possible? We stop all judgments and refuse to think judgmentally about one another. We accept our church leadership and accept each other and trust that God will make whatever adjustments need to be made and rest in that belief.

Now look at this reference about what Paul said to the Corinthians:

<u>1 Cor 1:10</u> *Now I plead with you, brethren, by the name of our Lord Jesus Christ, that you all speak the same thing, and that*

there be no divisions among you, but that you be perfectly joined together in the same mind and in the same judgment.

For this to be possible we must give up all claims to our own rights and opinions. We must keep ourselves down to the basics and learn how to respond to the opportunities of God as they present themselves to us. Then as we move forward we do so carefully and with all humility and humbleness of heart and mind.

Look how strongly Paul appeals to the Philippian church:

<u>Phil 1:27</u> *Only let your conduct be worthy of the gospel of Christ, so that whether I come and see you or am absent, I may hear of your affairs, that you stand fast in one spirit, with one mind striving together for the faith of the gospel,*

The word conduct means lifestyle. So Paul is calling them to live a lifestyle that is in keeping with the word of God. That then the church would be a group of people who stand fast, meaning they won't move off of being one in spirit. Then they would be of one mind, which connotes agreement that they lay down any differences and choose to agree. While in the course of church life much of our decision making gets done on an emotional level the key is that we would make our decisions in that place where our mind and will reside and dominate. We would not give in to our emotions but that we again would make the choice to be in agreement. This agreement takes precedence over our perceived personal rights and opinions.

See how Paul demands they think of one another:

<u>Phil 2:4, 5</u> *Let each of you look out not only for his own interests, but also for the interests of others. Let this mind be in you which was also in Christ Jesus*

The point is that the more important place to live is that place that what is in the best interests of the whole is more important that what is in my best interests. If we stop and think about it this is how Jesus lived. He had the right to demand every accommodation and comfort in his life on earth but instead He gave up what is rightly his and came to serve us and humble himself and gave his life for us.

These are attitudes and viewpoints to strive for in each of our local churches!

DISCUSSION CHAPTER NINE
PETER "SENT"

1) What did Philip accomplish in Samaria?

2) What was Peter and John sent to do as a follow up?

3) How did Peter and John accomplish this?

4) Describe the importance of impartation and what it means?

5) Describe the importance of being sent?

6) Describe the importance of agreement in the local church?

CHAPTER TEN
PETER HEALING THE SICK AND
RAISING THE DEAD

<u>Acts 9:32-43</u> *Now it came to pass, as Peter went through all PARTS OF THE COUNTRY, that he also came down to the saints who dwelt in Lydda. There he found a certain man named Aeneas, who had been bedridden eight years and was paralyzed. And Peter said to him, "Aeneas, Jesus the Christ heals you. Arise and make your bed." Then he arose immediately. So all who dwelt at Lydda and Sharon saw him and turned to the Lord.*

At Joppa there was a certain disciple named Tabitha, which is translated Dorcas. This woman was full of good works and charitable deeds which she did. But it happened in those days that she became sick and died. When they had washed her, they laid HER in an upper room. And since Lydda was near Joppa, and the disciples had heard that Peter was there, they sent two men to him, imploring HIM not to delay in coming to them. Then Peter arose and went with them. When he had come, they brought HIM to the upper room. And all the widows stood by him weeping, showing the tunics and garments which Dorcas had made while she was with them.

But Peter put them all out, and knelt down and prayed. And turning to the body he said, "Tabitha, arise." And she opened her eyes, and when she saw Peter she sat up. Then he gave her HIS hand and lifted her up; and when he had called the saints and widows, he presented her alive. And it became known throughout all Joppa, and many believed on the Lord. So it was that he stayed many days in Joppa with Simon, a tanner.

First let's consider the healing of Aeneas; he was a man bedridden for eight years. Notice the authority applied by Peter to this man's condition. He said Jesus Christ – "maketh thee whole." So Peter applied the present power available to every believer – in the present tense – Jesus is making you whole right now! Then Peter says make your bed and get up, and Aeneas obeyed and got up immediately – healed.

<u>Is. 53:5</u> *But He was wounded for our transgressions, He was bruised for our iniquities; The chastisement for our peace was upon Him, And by His stripes we are healed.*

Let us note that sickness and disease as a human experience requires a payment. This means there is an obligation involved that has mystified us in our human experience. Sickness and disease were not a part of the original intention of God. But with sin came the hurts that life can bring. In order for those things to be healed there is a requirement that only God can fulfill. That requirement as a part of the Master Plan for humanity is that the suffering of Jesus would pay in full the obligation that which was required as a result of sin on earth. Note what God said in the garden.

<u>Gen 2:17</u> *but of the tree of the knowledge of good and evil you shall not eat, for in the day that you eat of it you shall surely die."*

This spoke of an instant "death of the spirit" for Adam and for all mankind. It must be noted that sin brought upon the earth all sickness, disease, temptations, murder, lying and all the other actions in life that lead to death of the body.

Here the Bible shows us how that payment was made; it was "by His stripes we are healed." Consider the significance of the fact that about seven hundred years prior to the crucifixion and the actual event prophesied in Is. 53, that there was a present application (seven hundred years before the crucifixion) to the healing power of Christ. We must understand that based on a future activity promised by God through His prophet that present power was available for the benefits of that promise.

1 Peter 2:24 *who Himself bore our sins in His own body on the tree, that we, having died to sins, might live for righteousness— by whose stripes you were healed.*

We see here that Peter wrote by His stripes "you were healed." So prophetically speaking in Isaiah he declared that there was a present application based on a promised future event – as in the future sacrifice of Jesus. Likewise, after the fact of the suffering of Christ – that there is a present and future application based on what Christ has done for us in the past. The provision for healing has already taken place and Jesus does not need to do anything additional on our behalf!

This means that physical healing has always been in the plan and heart of God. For some reason the church wants to keep debating the gift of healing – when it has always been a part of our relationship with Him. Evidently people keep trying to figure out why some people don't get healed and so they want to construct a theology around the time it doesn't happen.

All too often we have heard said, "It must be God's will that they did not get healed." Or another common thing said is "that God must be trying to teach them something." There is not one Biblical example that either one of these statements can be true. He has provided for healing through the suffering of His son. So, for God to USE sickness as a tool in working with believers is an absolutely absurd proposition. Again we are trying to justify the mystery of sickness and why some get sick and not healed.

It can happen that we draw closer to God when sick – but that is often because the things of this earth quickly grow faintly dim and suddenly do not matter like they did to us the day before we got sick.

We live in a sinful world. There is a grace of God that enables us to live on this earth. While we wait for the second coming of Christ there are some things that happen that are hard to understand. There are things that happen that are not from the desire of God. The devil does his work and there are many cause and effects at work that we may not understand. But regardless of what we don't understand we can rest assured that God's will for us is to be healed. We need to tap into that truth, hold onto it, believe it, and not be dismayed by what we may see with our natural eyes that appears to be a contradiction.

Now let's go back to our original passage in Acts 9 when the ladies of Joppa prevailed upon Peter.

This is a most interesting account of the release of the Power of God through a believer. First of all it seems that not all believers know how to tap into the use of the Power of God.

Let's be clear all believers have the power to lay hands on the sick for them to be healed. But at the same time there is the "gifts of healing."

<u>1 Cor 12:9</u> *to another faith by the same Spirit, to another gifts of healings by the same Spirit,*

Notice there is the word "gifts" in the plural. It seems that there are those people in certain times that have a special infilling of the Holy Spirit that enables them to operate in the gifts of healing in extraordinary fashion or circumstances.

It may not be good exegesis to say what I am about to say – but let me submit a thought that reduces the mystery surrounding the gifts of healing for me. We have some people in the Kingdom of God here on earth that have the faith to preach to thousands of people and see thousands saved. The fact is – technically we all "can" do this. But we don't all do it, because we do not get ourselves into the situations that enable such events to take place.

It seems with all gifting from God there are times and places and people all coming together to make things happen to advance the Kingdom of God. I have observed that just as in the medical community there are specialists for heart, lungs, back, kidney, and other parts of the body, there are often in the faith community those that pray and believe for certain or specific kinds of healing and not for others.

In other words, there is the plural gift of healing available in the church. Not all people flow in all of those "gifts," but it is a valid form of expression of the heart of the Father for His church. Consider that Jesus during His ministry time on earth never once said healing is not the will of God in the 19 specific times he healed people prior to his suffering. Likewise we do not see one example of failed healing as the Apostles ramped up the early church. If it were ever NOT the will of God to heal would He not give us one example for us to see that there are exceptions?

Maybe an event that will help us better understand this was when Jesus went to the pool of Bethesda. He surly walked over many sick people to get to the man the Father wanted healed. When Jesus said, "take up your bed and walk," the man surly did. But others there did not.

It seems that as we walk in the "Spirit" with God that his leading will put emphasis on our ministry form and expression. It further seems that we can "tap into" certain gifting modes and we practice them and become proficient in how they operate through us. The more times we see the gifting operate through us the more success we will have in giving expression of the gift. I think there may be certain types of healing that some people have more faith for than others. Some people readily have faith for headaches to be healed or sore backs to be healed. It does not mean they don't pray for all healing but they have a "special faith" that if they pray for a certain ailment that God will use them to heal it.

It was perceived by the women of Joppa that Peter could tap into the resurrection power of God. The women sent a delegation to impose upon Peter to come to them. Dorcas was a famous woman whose claim to fame was that she "had been full of good works, and alms deeds." This means she was a woman who cared and did for others – and did it on a notable scale.

Dorcas was dead when they sent for Peter! When Peter came – at least a day or so later – they were all weeping and showing Peter evidence of the things she had sewed for others. Now if you stop and think about it – these friends of Dorcas had heard of the healing power available in the life of a man called Peter. They had the audacity to prevail upon Peter for their dead friend. Peter (nor God) could resist the faith and audacity to appeal for such intervention for their friend and loved one. This is a point also lost on the general western church. We need faith to ask and the courage to prevail upon God to come into our life's situations. These people could not find the faith to raise her from the dead within themselves but they knew where that kind of faith was and they sent for it – in a man called Peter.

Peter (like Jesus had done), sent everyone out of the room and prayed for her. Remember get rid of all potential doubt and unbelief. Peter called out her name and told her to rise and she did! Resurrection came to Dorcas and salvation came to the city of Joppa.

Is it not a grand thing in the Kingdom of God that noteworthy servants can receive special treatment? Is it not wonderful that friends can come together and prevail upon God and His chosen servants for a friend? Isn't it wonderful that for the second time already in the early life of the church that those who cared for others and particularly the poor were eligible to receive intervention from God?

This city of Joppa needed its own introduction to the faith and God chose neither the government officials nor the religious officials of the area to bring faith. He chose a woman named Dorcas. Her name is the name of a kind of a Gazelle. The Dorcas Gazelle is not the smallest Gazelle – but it is small. The Dorcas Gazelle is not the most common of the species – but it is common. Imagine the kind of God and what it reflects about His heart, who selects a relatively small and common woman who spent countless hours sewing garments for those less fortunate to demonstrate the resurrection power of Jesus. This demonstration brought salvation to the whole region as a result of this resurrection, which is a manifestation of the love of God on earth.

For God so loved the world that He gave His only begotten Son.

DISCUSSION CHAPTER TEN
PETER HEALING THE SICK AND RAISING THE DEAD

1) What happened in the communities around Aeneas and Dorcas after their encounter with healing and resurrection?

2) Is there ever a Biblical example of God specifically refusing to heal?

3) What was the impact of God's promise that the suffering of Christ would "provide" for healing?

4) Who has the right to pray for healing?

5) How would you describe the "gifts of healing?"

CHAPTER ELEVEN
PETER CHOSEN AS AN INSTRUMENT OF TRANSITION

Acts 10:9-17 *The next day, as they went on their journey and drew near the city, Peter went up on the housetop to pray, about the sixth hour. Then he became very hungry and wanted to eat; but while they made ready, he fell into a trance and saw heaven opened and an object like a great sheet bound at the four corners, descending to him and let down to the earth. In it were all kinds of four-footed animals of the earth, wild beasts, creeping things, and birds of the air. And a voice came to him, "Rise, Peter; kill and eat."*

But Peter said, "Not so, Lord! For I have never eaten anything common or unclean." And a voice SPOKE to him again the second time, "What God has cleansed you must not call common." This was done three times. And the object was taken up into heaven again.

Now while Peter wondered within himself what this vision which he had seen meant, behold, the men who had been sent from Cornelius had made inquiry for Simon's house, and stood before the gate. And they called and asked whether Simon, whose surname was Peter, was lodging there.

It is often difficult for us to understand each other when it comes to religious training or methods of expression used in our interactive relationship with our God. The Jews at the time of Peter had been without any new written books from God for over four hundred years. During these years teachings had become pretty dogmatic, especially those that separated Jews from those that called on other gods.

Actually under the Old Covenant there were strict rules of eating, and at the same time they began to proclaim somewhere along the line that there were only certain people that you could eat with. As we know from Jesus' time on earth that He kept challenging the conventional religious wisdom that it was emphasizing the wrong things all the time.

But now God wanted to more directly change the paradigm about both food and people. Under the Old Covenant people had to become a converted Jew, meeting all the requirements of circumcision and memorization and the like. Well the early church ASSUMED that Christians had to be converted into a Jew and then become a Christian. The confusion is understandable and the need for a powerful testimony to transition this thinking was planned by God.

There had been quite a distinctive in Jewish teachings that dealt with eating including what kind of foods were to be eaten as well as how these foods were prepared. Not unlike in my younger years Catholics were not to eat meat on Friday. They had to eat fish and this rule for eating was a common point of distinction and pressure in the life of the adherents.

Peter was faced with a vision that painfully struck all these eating sensibilities that had been ingrained in him his whole life. Note Peter was very hungry and was actually in a trance. This type of communicative vision from God is a method that is utilized by God occasionally with key believers who are continually seeking Him and relating with Him. A vision is like

God pulling back the veil between the dimension of heaven and the dimension of earth.

Even during the vision Peter knows this was not a temptation coming from the devil, but was in fact the Lord offering to Peter those things Peter grew up believing he was not allowed to have. But as God's gifts are ever expanding His restraints are ever loosening. It is also of note that the vision repeated 3 times. This seems to be the way God could get through to him to get Peter's buy in.

While Peter argued with God (!), the Lord did not upbraid him for the argument. But God introduced a change in theology- a transition into the New Covenant. The Lord clearly says that He has now called these animals clean – therefore they are now clean and you can eat them. You see it matters not what our perceptions are it matters what God says.

God was going to use Peter to be a vessel for change. It was not just a matter of changing eating rules. There was another more significant change that was coming with the New Covenant. You see Jesus was now expanding His relationships quickly beyond the limitations of historical Jewish thinking. The Old Covenant was geared toward the Jews to be an example of God working with a people group. And others were invited in to become a part of the Jewish nation and therefore in relationship with God.

But now God was breaking through to Peter by changing the eating rules to expand Peter's thinking so he would be open to the real change. The real change the Father was going for was a new definition of who are the People of God. We have to see that this was a major confrontation with all those things held important by people who had already been living for God in the way they had been raised. They were dedicated to how they had been trained and taught to serve. Peter was being asked to transition to a new way of looking at food and looking at people and it was pretty overwhelming. Let's face it, have you ever argued with God? Peter did in this trance!

Notice Peter came out of the trance wondering what on earth that was all about. But as we will see below the timing was magnificent.

PART 2

Acts 10:14-48 *While Peter thought about the vision, the Spirit said to him, "Behold, three men are seeking you. Arise therefore, go down and go with them, doubting nothing; for I have sent them."*

Then Peter went down to the men who had been sent to him from Cornelius, and said, "Yes, I am he whom you seek. For what reason have you come?"

And they said, "Cornelius THE centurion, a just man, one who fears God and has a good reputation among all the nation of the Jews, was divinely instructed by a holy angel to summon you to his house, and to hear words from you." Then he invited them in and lodged THEM.

On the next day Peter went away with them, and some brethren from Joppa accompanied him. And the following day they entered Caesarea. Now Cornelius was waiting for them, and had called together his relatives and close friends. As Peter was coming in, Cornelius met him and fell down at his feet and worshiped HIM. But Peter lifted him up, saying, "Stand up; I myself am also a man." And as he talked with him, he went in and found many who had come together. Then he said to them, "You know how unlawful it is for a Jewish man to keep company with or go to one of another nation. But God has shown me that I should not call any man common or unclean. Therefore I came without objection as soon as I was sent for. I ask, then, for what reason have you sent for me?"

So Cornelius said, "Four days ago I was fasting until this hour; and at the ninth hour I prayed in my house, and behold, a man stood before me in bright clothing, and said, 'Cornelius, your prayer has been heard, and your alms are remembered in the sight of God. Send therefore to Joppa and call Simon here, whose surname is Peter. He is lodging in the house of Simon, a tanner, by the sea. When he comes, he will speak to you.' So I sent to you immediately, and you have done well to come. Now therefore, we are all present before God, to hear all the things commanded you by God."

Then Peter opened HIS mouth and said: "In truth I perceive that God shows no partiality. But in every nation whoever fears Him and works righteousness is accepted by Him. The word which GOD sent to the children of Israel, preaching peace through Jesus Christ—He is Lord of all— that word you know, which was proclaimed throughout all Judea, and began from Galilee after the baptism which John preached: how God anointed Jesus of Nazareth with the Holy Spirit and with power, who went about doing good and healing all who were oppressed by the devil, for God was with Him. And we are witnesses of all things which He did both in the land of the Jews and in Jerusalem, whom they killed by hanging on a tree. Him God raised up on the third day, and showed Him openly, not to all the people, but to witnesses chosen before by God, EVEN to us who ate and drank with Him after He arose from the dead. And He commanded us to preach to the people, and to testify that it is He who was ordained by God TO BE Judge of the living and the dead. To Him all the prophets witness that, through His name, whoever believes in Him will receive remission of sins."

While Peter was still speaking these words, the Holy Spirit fell upon all those who heard the word. And those of the circumcision who believed were astonished, as many as came with Peter, because the gift of the Holy Spirit had been poured out on the Gentiles also. For they heard them speak with tongues and magnify God.

Then Peter answered, "Can anyone forbid water, that these should not be baptized who have received the Holy Spirit just as we HAVE?" And he commanded them to be baptized in the name of the Lord. Then they asked him to stay a few days.

Before we talk about the transition for the church let's take a moment and consider Cornelius. He of course was a gentile (Italian) and had authority to command one hundred men unto their death in battle. But he began seeking God perhaps because he had heard of the stories of the resurrection of the man Jesus who was crucified by one of his fellow soldiers.

It is interesting that he had developed a method and plan to find this God! He fasted, so he knew God wanted men in control of their appetites. He prayed so he knew somehow that God heard prayers. He gave alms so he understood the compassion of God for the poor. It was a powerful testimony when the angel came to him and said his prayers and alms were **noticed by God.** We should better understand this God we serve. He takes note of our actions. Our actions influence His response! God hears about our help for the poor and puts it on the "to do list for His angels!" God was taken with this man and his heart – an occupier of the land of Israel, holding the Jewish nation under rule – but who cared for the Jewish people by helping those in need.

Well, let's move on to the church transition being affected here:

Peter was the man God was using to unfold the profile of the New Covenant. Peter had quickly come into the revelation of the bold new expression of the goodness of God. But without further direction during the first few days and weeks after Pentecost the usual teaching was first become a Jew then become a Christian. After all the initial converts were Jews so nothing in their common thinking seemed to affect any change. Up until this time the Jews were not even supposed to eat with Gentiles.

Peter grasped that his vision hours before was to shift his own paradigm - that salvation was for anyone and everyone who would believe. That not only was God changing what he called unclean now clean in the animal kingdom, but that now salvation was to be made available to all who would call upon the Name of Jesus. While Peter preached he and his witnesses saw with their own eyes that the whole group of Gentiles were getting saved and baptized in the Holy Spirit. (As a side light, notice they were baptized into the Holy Spirit prior to water baptism-just when we think we have it figured out God does things a different way!). They realized that God was working in new ways and was changing eating habits and adding people groups to the covenant all in one fell swoop.

We must see that this was a paradigm shift the likes of which man had not previously been challenged with. It is important to understand that the common belief system that ruled the Old Covenant was now being undermined. It seems that God was introducing the reality of "whom the Son sets free is free indeed."

Down through history we can look back and see that God introduced further revelation of Himself in waves if you will. As an example, consider this conversation God had with Moses;

Exodus 6:2, 3 *And God spoke to Moses and said to him: "I AM the LORD. I appeared to Abraham, to Isaac, and to Jacob, as God Almighty, but BY My name LORD I was not known to them.*

So we see that as generations go by and as times and seasons move on there is different emphasis of God's nature that is revealed. As already said He is overwhelming in all His glory. The change from the Old to the New was so severe that it would take thoughtful people with an open heart and a seeking mind to move with God during the change.

If you stop and think about it when a wave comes on to the shore and releases its white cap to run up on the sand and rocks that it immediately flows back to the ocean and brings resistance to the next wave that is coming on shore. This is historically true in man's relationship with God. God was known as "God Almighty" to Abraham, Isaac, and Jacob, but now the revelation of Jehovah was coming. He was not going to overpower Egypt or Pharaoh as Almighty, but He was going to defeat the Egyptian belief system by defeating the works of their gods one by one.

Amazingly the father of our faith – Abraham – we are told had a limited understanding and relationship with God. Yet we see how faith guided Abraham even with that limitation. God was telling Moses that Moses was being granted more understanding of God. There is not an example of the contrary in the Bible. I mean that there is no example where God revealed Himself to one generation and then with held that revelation from the next generation. God is always progressively unfolding Himself.

Since Jesus came and lived and died and rose again from the dead we have seen God revealed in the flesh and His love revealed in our hearts. Now with the Holy Spirit we are enabled to see and hear from God individually and personally. We actually are enabled to know God like the prophets of old strained to get a glimpse of without ever doing it. Knowing this our obligation to walk in this revelation in holiness is higher than any previous generation.

Back to Peter now, we see that Peter was the instrument for change. He went to visit Cornelius with 6 other Jewish believers. Interestingly this was twice the number of witnesses legally required to testify the truth of a matter.

I can see Peter now looking with amazement on the house of Cornelius as they were saved and baptized in the Holy Spirit and per his direction then baptized with water. Rejoicing in all of this and yet knowing that he must answer to the other apostles. The other disciples and apostles did not have the benefit of a vision nor the witness of what happened with Cornelius. The group was still small enough that anyone going off on their own was going to have to answer to the group. Peter or no Peter, apostle or no apostle, agreement was a cornerstone of the early church.

Word of the Cornelius event beat Peter back to Jerusalem. Interestingly, Peter rehearsed with his Jewish witnesses all the way back to Jerusalem the sequence of events. I am sure they were trying to keep their story straight as to how this was a "God thing" and not something they just did on their own.

This new wave of revelation was going to be strongly resisted by the previous wave. Just anyone coming to salvation on their own was contrary to all religious thinking. There is, in our human rationale, a tendency to try to add new truth onto our previous understandings. In other words, their religious thinking had been for 1500 years, that a Gentile could become a Jew, but only according to a certain procedure. The Gentile must come into the community and observe all of the Jewish customs and practices as laid out by both the Bible and the Talmud.

Then the males had to be circumcised and then they would be accepted as Jewish converts. Now the thinking was that the same procedure would apply. But Jesus did not die on the cross and rise from the dead to become an addendum to the Old Covenant. He came to bring a New Covenant- a new agreement between God and man. He came to bridge the gap from God to man. It had been proven that man left to his own could not find his way to God.

So very quickly God opened this revelation to Peter to present to the other apostles to deal with this truth quickly and decisively. Now when we look back at the ministry of Jesus on earth we can see why he continually attacked the "thinking and behavior patterns" of the religious leaders. They had reduced their religion to following outward activities while their hearts were far from God. They had actually built a religious system that required their services to be used by the people to get access to God.

Jesus, by His death and resurrection had torn down everything that stands in the way between God and man. God became instantly accessible to a person who would "confess their sins with their mouth and believe in their heart that Jesus saved them."

Thank God every believer has access to the throne of Grace. We do not serve a system we serve a Person and His Name is Jesus. We do not have a series of meaningless rules to follow, our access is assured, our appeal has power, and His care is certain.

DISCUSSION CHAPTER ELEVEN
PETER CHOSEN AS AN INSTRUMENT OF TRANSITION

1) Considering the dietary laws of the Old Covenant, interpret the dream that Peter had – in detail.

2) Why would Peter argue with God?

3) What was God's final word on the subject?

4) How did Cornelius get God's attention?

5) What do you think about an individual "getting God's attention?" Does God play favorites?

6) The Spirit told Peter to go with the strangers at the door and he obeyed immediately. What was Peter's demeanor arriving at the house of Cornelius?

CHAPTER TWELVE
PETER BRINGS THE PARADIGM SHIFT TO THE REST OF THE LEADERS

<u>Acts 11:1-18</u> *Now the apostles and brethren who were in Judea heard that the Gentiles had also received the word of God. And when Peter came up to Jerusalem, those of the circumcision contended with him, saying, "You went in to uncircumcised men and ate with them!"*

But Peter explained IT to them in order from the beginning, saying: "I was in the city of Joppa praying; and in a trance I saw a vision, an object descending like a great sheet, let down from heaven by four corners; and it came to me. When I observed it intently and considered, I saw four-footed animals of the earth, wild beasts, creeping things, and birds of the air. And I heard a voice saying to me, 'Rise, Peter; kill and eat.' But I said, 'Not so, Lord! For nothing common or unclean has at any time entered my mouth.' But the voice answered me again from heaven, 'What God has cleansed you must not call common.' Now this was done three times, and all were drawn up again into heaven.

At that very moment, three men stood before the house where I was, having been sent to me from Caesarea. Then the Spirit told me to go with them, doubting nothing. Moreover these six brethren accompanied me, and we entered the man's house. And he told us how he had seen an angel standing in his house, who said to him, 'Send men to Joppa, and call for Simon whose surname is Peter, who will tell you words by which you and all your household will be saved.' And as I began to speak, the

Holy Spirit fell upon them, as upon us at the beginning. Then I remembered the word of the Lord, how He said, 'John indeed baptized with water, but you shall be baptized with the Holy Spirit.' If therefore God gave them the same gift as HE GAVE us when we believed on the Lord Jesus Christ, who was I that I could withstand God?"

When they heard these things they became silent; and they glorified God, saying, "Then God has also granted to the Gentiles repentance to life."

It is almost funny that their first contention among the leadership of the early church was over the fact that Peter and the six Jewish believers went to **eat with** Cornelius and his household! Praise be to God that what could have been continued contention and even separation became instead a place of praise among the leadership of the early church. Salvation brings openness to the hearts of people who are so grateful for their own salvation that they can rejoice whenever God reaches out to the unlikely to be saved.

When we come to grips with the fact that as an individual I am undeserving and sinful. When we acknowledge that each of us has failed yet God by His mercy has come and provided the payment required saving us. We then should become very tolerant and open to all others that He has saved. While it is very easy to claim others may be worse the point is we are not qualified to draw the line. In fact when we realize that once you have broken one law you have broken all laws we see that there is no line to be drawn.

The passage above is not the end of the matter. A few years later the issue boiled over again as more Jews were converted and went out preaching to the Gentiles and they had not been instructed how to accommodate gentile converts. So they were saying that you had to enter the Old Covenant first – the circumcision – in order to get saved. Now understand that the "Cornelius decision" had been made but evidently not well published. On the other hand it takes a revelation to move into this paradigm shift for Jewish believers.

As more Jewish converts took up the Cause of Christ it was not a part of their thinking yet. A more formal decision and a written proclamation needed to be implemented for all that were added to the church in those days. As we look at the following passage of scripture we will see that from among the Jews there were converts coming into the faith and yet maintaining their Jewish sect as a point of recognition. These in fact could be considered the first expression of "denominations." A denomination is nothing more than a group of people that identify themselves as belonging together over their own emphasis of teaching in the faith.

We have today people that identify together over methods of water baptizing. We have people gathered together over methods of Biblical interpretation, over Baptism in the Holy Spirit, over dress codes, and over segregation of core beliefs about things like the second coming of Christ.

Peter took up the first argument in the court of the believing leadership and now again a few years after the Cornelius ruling:

<u>Acts 15:5-11</u> *But some of the sect of the Pharisees who believed rose up, saying, "It is necessary to circumcise them, and to command THEM to keep the law of Moses."*

Now the apostles and elders came together to consider this matter. And when there had been much dispute, Peter rose up AND said to them: "Men AND brethren, you know that a good while ago God chose among us, that by my mouth the Gentiles should hear the word of the gospel and believe. So God, who knows the heart, acknowledged them by giving them the Holy Spirit, just as HE DID to us, and made no distinction between us and them, purifying their hearts by faith. Now therefore, why do you test God by putting a yoke on the neck of the disciples which neither our fathers nor we were able to bear? But we believe that through the grace of the Lord Jesus Christ we shall be saved in the same manner as they."

So Peter pleaded the case for grace. In fact his argument was compelling as he closed with the fact that neither they nor their fathers were able to live up to the Old Covenant- why then would they require Gentiles to go through that door first?

Then Paul and Barnabas took up the argument and the session closed with a written report that laid out four things that were expected of the Gentiles:

<u>Acts 15:20</u> *but that we write to them to abstain from things polluted by idols, FROM sexual immorality, FROM things strangled, and FROM blood.*

No where were these demands ever brought up again. They were not enforced per se upon the Gentiles, but it brought comfort because all could agree that whether Jew or Gentile converting to Christianity that these were 4 things that should be dealt with in the context of the cultures of the day.

The message is clear – **Jesus plus anything is nothing!** Customs and rules and regulations add nothing to our salvation. Our outward behavior can never be good enough to attain salvation. Our group identity can be acceptable to God – He is flexible on what we may emphasize. But as I told someone famous one time – God does not grade on a curve. You are either in (with faith in Jesus) or you are out (when you don't accept His payment for your sins). He will usually leave the door to faith open to the last moment. The problem is you cannot predict that last moment and you may not have a voice or thought in your last moment.

DISCUSSION CHAPTER TWELVE
PETER BRINGS THE PARADIGM SHIFT TO THE REST OF THE LEADERS:

1) Why would this issue come up again?

2) Can we see a common thread with people today who invite others to join their denomination?

3) From your background what have you thought people needed to do to be saved?

4) What do you think about the 4 rules that were written down and published?

5) What does it mean "by grace are you saved through faith?"

CHAPTER THIRTEEN
PETER EXPERIENCES SUPERNATURAL
ANGELIC INTERVENTION

<u>Acts 12:1-18</u> *Now about that time Herod the king stretched out HIS hand to harass some from the church. Then he killed James the brother of John with the sword. And because he saw that it pleased the Jews, he proceeded further to seize Peter also. Now it was DURING the Days of Unleavened Bread. So when he had arrested him, he put HIM in prison, and delivered HIM to four squads of soldiers to keep him, intending to bring him before the people after Passover.*

Peter was therefore kept in prison, but constant prayer was offered to God for him by the church. And when Herod was about to bring him out, that night Peter was sleeping, bound with two chains between two soldiers; and the guards before the door were keeping the prison. Now behold, an angel of the Lord stood by HIM, and a light shone in the prison; and he struck Peter on the side and raised him up, saying, "Arise quickly!" And his chains fell off HIS hands.

Then the angel said to him, "Gird yourself and tie on your sandals"; and so he did. And he said to him, "Put on your garment and follow me." So he went out and followed him, and did not know that what was done by the angel was real, but thought he was seeing a vision. When they were past the first and the second guard posts, they came to the iron gate that leads to the city, which opened to them of its own accord; and they went out and went down one street, and immediately the angel departed from him.

And when Peter had come to himself, he said, "Now I know for certain that the Lord has sent His angel, and has delivered me from the hand of Herod and FROM all the expectation of the Jewish people."

So, when he had considered THIS, he came to the house of Mary, the mother of John whose surname was Mark, where many were gathered together praying. And as Peter knocked at the door of the gate, a girl named Rhoda came to answer. When she recognized Peter's voice, because of HER gladness she did not open the gate, but ran in and announced that Peter stood before the gate. But they said to her, "You are beside yourself!" Yet she kept insisting that it was so. So they said, "It is his angel."

Now Peter continued knocking; and when they opened THE DOOR and saw him, they were astonished. But motioning to them with his hand to keep silent, he declared to them how the Lord had brought him out of the prison. And he said, "Go, tell these things to James and to the brethren." And he departed and went to another place.

Then, as soon as it was day, there was no small stir among the soldiers about what had become of Peter.

Just prior to the last mention of Peter in the book of Acts we see that Peter was involved in a bizarre angelic intervention.

Bizarre to us because the vast majority of us have never had an angel manifestation experience that we know of. If we look at the various supernatural manifestations revealed in the Book of Acts, we see that Peter participated in all of them! So we can understand that the obsessive compulsive nature of Peter was the kind of person that looked for and expected these kinds of happenings. At least let us realize that everything that happened to Peter can happen to us.

Now let's give this further discussion. Peter never tried to conjure up the Spirit. So often the church comes together in this day and worships God trying to "get God" to show Himself in some recognizable fashion. We don't see that in Peter in any of his worship. What we see is a man who loves and worships God with his whole heart trusting God to be with him and allowing God to have His good pleasure.

What this means is that Peter was never in a meeting where he was trying to make the Presence of God a manifested reality. He was either seeking God or praising God with all his heart. He was not trying to get God to get him out of jail. He was chained up and trusting God. Jesus was his God if He never did another thing for Peter.

1 Peter 2:9 *But you are a chosen generation, a royal priesthood, a holy nation, His own special people, that you may proclaim the praises of Him who called you out of darkness into His marvelous light;*

Peter found himself able to get in the flow with the Spirit of God. He had sensitivity to the Holy Spirit and was able to take His direction and follow His every inspiration. Peter thought he was seeing a vision when the Angel was leading him out of prison. He was walking in the Spirit and consider the fact that his chains, which were attached to two jailers next to him, were unlocked and he got up and got dressed and at the urging of the Angel, hurried and walked out of there.

We must realize that we live in a world on this earth that is separate but connected to the Kingdom of God. The Kingdom of God reaches through the separated dimension via the Spirit. There is the prayer Jesus taught – on earth as it is in heaven – meaning that via prayer and the working of the Holy Spirit connecting with our spirit and via His word, what was wanted to be done on earth was possible.

Let's consider a current practical example that may help us understand better how this connection takes place. Radio has been a revolutionary medium in the history of the industrial revolution. It was at the heart of communication as more households bought a radio and would sit around it at night and listen to their favorite programs. President Roosevelt used the radio for his "fireside chats" during the Second World War. This is an odd picture to this current generation but it was an important means of communication by long distance that was novel and exciting at the time.

There were limitations on radio including the inability to see the speakers, but more importantly there was a limitation to the distance away from the broadcaster. Most stations have a limited geographic reach unless their signal is boosted locally.

A few years ago along came an all new radio technology. Two companies put satellites into space and they transmit programming across the entire United States. Where ever you drive you can hear the channel and same program regardless of geography or travel. The geographic limitation has been eliminated. Now the satellite companies required a special antenna and special receiver in order to hear their broadcast. Normal radios cannot pick up the signal.

Peter as well as all of us as believers have the antenna and receiver (our spirit), to pick up the broadcast from heaven. But we must turn it on and tune it in to get on the right channel. Peter tuned into God under the duress of sitting chained in prison. Heaven (God) took notice that the prayers of the church and the praise going forth from the heart of the man and chose to intervene with an Angel to deliver Peter.

When Peter was at the gate beautiful he tuned in – he fastened his eyes on the beggar listening for God's inspiration. Even before that he tuned in to hear that the roar in the upper room was what Joel had prophesied. So he got up and preached it.

Each encounter of healing and raising the dead and breaking the eating laws of the Jews were inspired responses from Peter tuning into the heavenly broadcast. Most of us labor under our own agenda and are too busy speaking and not spending enough time listening. This is the extent of our communication with heaven. Peter was the man example in the beginning days of the church that set forth a new paradigm that when we tune in to God that He will lead us and guide us and use us! But we must be flexible and ready to go. He does not often tell us what to do tomorrow, usually the inspiration is for today.

Now back to our text; there was a political move afoot by Herod who as all politicians seeks how they can find the favor of the people. Even for those people subjugated by the Romans it was always good to find their favor as less trouble would be caused by them, thus further securing Herod's political position. All through history we find that occupying forces, while in control, try to find some level of civility to improve the cooperation of the host country populace. So when the leader could curry favor by making a decision that was of no consequence to the invaders he would do it, so he could make his demands more acceptable.

Herod had killed James the brother of John and had received favorable "press" among the ruling Jewish leadership. So he thought he would continue this method of securing further favor by securing another "leader" among the rebellious upstart Jewish Christians and likewise killing him. So he had Peter arrested and was on his way to meet him at prison and have him killed.

But Peter was nowhere to be found so Herod killed the prison keepers. He did not want to appear weak so he couldn't take the risk of trying to send out a search party for Peter. That could take days or weeks and thus Herod would lose political ground gained. So he had the guards killed and traveled to the next city. He was becoming full of himself and God literally struck him dead as the people called him a god and he would not deny it.

Politics and God are virtually always at odds. But thanks be to God that the church can find effectiveness, power and change when they are in agreement in prayer. It is clear that the prayers of the saints released into action the move of a delivering angel. This angelic account also reveals the "spiritual dimension" that walks alongside the natural dimension unseen and yet real. This is what we need to learn to tune into!

Notice when Peter knocked on the gate of the home where he knew the prayer meeting would be he was not immediately let in. When the young woman went back into the house to tell them Peter was at the gate, they assumed it was Peter's angel. What a strange assumption. Could it be that angels are more a part of our lives than we give credit for?

Hebrews 13:2 *Do not forget to entertain strangers, for by so doing some have unwittingly entertained angels.*

Now notice in our text that the people were "astonished" at his appearance at their home. Don't forget they were praying for this very thing. They knew that Herod was out to kill Peter. Let's look at this word astonished:

Astonished; Astonied: a(shamem, "astonished," the root idea being "silent," i.e. struck dumb with amazement; ekplessomai, "to be struck with astonishment," as if by a blow or a shock; existemi, "to amaze," "to throw into wonderment"; thambeomai, "to astonish" to the point of fright): The state of being surprised, startled, stunned by some exceptional wonder, some overwhelming event or miracle,

It was not that they were surprised their prayers were answered. Rather it was more like they were overcome by the power of God, seeing first hand for them that Jesus was alive and working with them as He had promised. It was a joy unspeakable event that Peter got out of a prison that there was no getting out of. This answered prayer against all odds – strengthened the church and empowered the people to go all the more boldly to their generation.

DISCUSSION CHAPTER THIRTEEN
PETER EXPERIENCES SUPERNATURAL ANGELIC
INTERVENTION

1) How could Peter walk out of prison without being caught?

2) Describe the heavenly dimension vs. the dimension we live in on earth.

3) How do we tune in to the heavenly dimension?

4) What do you think about angels, and why haven't you been aware of one?

Pratt, Dwight M. "Astonished;+Astonied," INTERNATIONAL STANDARD BIBLE ENCYCLOPAEDIA. Edited by James Orr. Blue Letter Bible. 1913. 1 Apr 2007. 26 Mar 2009

CHAPTER FOURTEEN
PETER IN THE EPISTLES OF PAUL

Galatians 2:6-16 *But from those who seemed to be something—whatever they were, it makes no difference to me; God shows personal favoritism to no man—for those who seemed TO BE SOMETHING added nothing to me. But on the contrary, when they saw that the gospel for the uncircumcised had been committed to me, as THE GOSPEL for the circumcised WAS to Peter (for He who worked effectively in Peter for the apostleship to the circumcised also worked effectively in me toward the Gentiles), and when James, Cephas, and John, who seemed to be pillars, perceived the grace that had been given to me, they gave me and Barnabas the right hand of fellowship, that we SHOULD GO to the Gentiles and they to the circumcised. THEY DESIRED only that we should remember the poor, the very thing which I also was eager to do.*

Now when Peter had come to Antioch, I withstood him to his face, because he was to be blamed; for before certain men came from James, he would eat with the Gentiles; but when they came, he withdrew and separated himself, fearing those who were of the circumcision. And the rest of the Jews also played the hypocrite with him, so that even Barnabas was carried away with their hypocrisy.

But when I saw that they were not straightforward about the truth of the gospel, I said to Peter before THEM all, "If you, being a Jew, live in the manner of Gentiles and not as the Jews, why do you compel Gentiles to live as Jews? We WHO ARE Jews by nature, and not sinners of the Gentiles, knowing that a man is not justified by the works of the law but by faith in Jesus Christ, even we have believed in Christ Jesus, that we might be justified by faith in Christ and not by the works of the law; for by the works of the law no flesh shall be justified.

Peter was still conflicted. He still struggled in eating with gentiles in the presence of other Jews.

Peter lived a conflicted life over the "Jewish issue." We have seen him experience a vision where God clearly spoke saying what God calls clean no man should call unclean. Peter took this revelation to apply not only to a new liberty to eat foods formerly deemed unclean; but he also took this revelation to apply to a new freedom for Gentiles to come into the faith – just as they are – and that it now was no longer necessary to have a rule against Jew and Gentile eating together.

We have seen Peter be the first to lead Gentiles into the saving knowledge of Jesus Christ. We have seen Peter argue before the apostolic leadership that Gentiles should not have to become Jews to get saved.

And now we see a few years later that it appeared that Peter was conflicted over the eating issue. It is reasonable to ask why? First of all let's see that on a personal level he was free in his own heart to eat with the Gentiles. This means that he personally was not conflicted. The conflict came over the perceptions of other Jewish believers. The church that Peter most associated with was Jewish converts. Each Jew who converted had to come to terms with the former eating laws and some took longer than others. In fact even today Jewish believers are free to decide for themselves if they want to observe the former eating laws. The issue comes down to the fact that we each have our own freedoms in these issues, but we do not have the right to impose our freedoms or our observances on others.

That while the decree had come down not to force gentiles to become Jews it had not come down specifically saying it was ok to eat with gentiles.

In our desire to get along with others even in leadership and even in the church we have a tendency to be restricted by what others think – right or wrong. Paul on the other hand was the most "learned" of the entire apostolic group. He was a trained theologian. He had the most training in school and was actually the most qualified in the ways of the Jewish laws. He knew the reasoning's and the ways of the Old Covenant most thoroughly of all the new leadership of the New Covenant.

In fact, Paul offered a compelling argument that he spent little time with the other apostles as he felt called to bring good theology to the upstart church of Jesus Christ. After Paul's salvation he spent as many as 17 years going through scripture revisiting old truths in the new light of Jesus as Messiah. So ambiguity was not going to be tolerated by Paul. He cared less of what the others thought; he was on an evangelistic mission to reach the world for Christ. He confronted dear Peter over his desire to be accepted by others saying the truth stands regardless of their approval.

The western church is mired in the need for approval by others and the perceptions of others. Perceptions and approval by man is the current plague upon the church and renders the church nearly impotent in America today. The church has little impact on the mores and social order of the day. We are accused of being dogmatic in this western culture when in fact the church seems to be doing nothing more but to complain about all of the social ills around us.

It is interesting that the seeds of being held in religious chains of perceptions and approval of others were in the very earliest leadership experiences of the church. In order to come into agreement today we force leaders to jump through hoops pleasing to men and not necessarily pleasing to God. Man somehow has elevated his opinions above his beliefs. Rather than being in sincere prayer seeking the mind and heart of God it seems that we are pleading for approval of our opinions by others.

Paul is pretty adamant that he had to have a face to face confrontation with Peter in front of others to further break this separation thinking among Jewish believers. It seems that he did not want this to slide under the rug. It was important to get this out in the open and have an open ruling about it. When a problem is revealed publicly the judgment needs be addressed publicly.

So Paul publically simply said, "You ate with Gentiles when no one from Jerusalem was here, but now that they are here you withdraw as if there was something wrong with them!"

So even though Peter was being sensitive to the Jewish believers he was being sensitive to their wrong beliefs that Jewish believers should not eat with Gentile believers.

Therefore his actions were unacceptable? We can assume that Paul's unanswered confrontation was the final word on the matter. We cannot foster separation among believers over trivial matters that are not sin.

Paul dealt with this topic in detail in the following letter to the **Romans 14**: *Receive one who is weak in the faith, BUT not to disputes over doubtful things. For one believes he may eat all things, but he who is weak eats ONLY vegetables. Let not him who eats despise him who does not eat, and let not him who does not eat judge him who eats; for God has received him. Who are you to judge another's servant? To his own master he stands or falls. Indeed, he will be made to stand, for God is able to make him stand.*

One person esteems ONE day above another; another esteems every day ALIKE. Let each be fully convinced in his own mind. He who observes the day, observes IT to the Lord; and he who does not observe the day, to the Lord he does not observe IT. He who eats, eats to the Lord, for he gives God thanks; and he who does not eat, to the Lord he does not eat, and gives God thanks. For none of us lives to himself, and no one dies to himself. For if we live, we live to the Lord; and if we die, we die to the Lord. Therefore, whether we live or die, we are the Lord's. For to this end Christ died and rose and lived again, that He might be Lord of both the dead and the living. But why do you judge your brother? Or why do you show contempt for your brother? For we shall all stand before the judgment seat of Christ. For it is written:

"AS I LIVE, SAYS THE LORD, EVERY KNEE SHALL BOW TO ME, AND EVERY TONGUE SHALL CONFESS TO GOD."

So then each of us shall give account of himself to God. Therefore let us not judge one another anymore, but rather resolve this, not to put a stumbling block or a cause to fall in OUR brother's way.

I know and am convinced by the Lord Jesus that THERE IS nothing unclean of itself; but to him who considers anything to be unclean, to him IT IS unclean. Yet if your brother is grieved because of YOUR food, you are no longer walking in love. Do not destroy with your food the one for whom Christ died. Therefore do not let your good be spoken of as evil; for the kingdom of God is not eating and drinking, but righteousness and peace and joy in the Holy Spirit. For he who serves Christ in these things IS acceptable to God and approved by men.

Therefore let us pursue the things WHICH MAKE for peace and the things by which one may edify another. Do not destroy the work of God for the sake of food. All things indeed ARE pure, but IT IS evil for the man who eats with offense. IT IS good neither to eat meat nor drink wine nor DO ANYTHING by which your brother stumbles or is offended or is made weak. Do you have faith? Have IT to yourself before God. Happy IS he who does not condemn himself in what he approves. But he who doubts is condemned if he eats, because HE DOES not EAT from faith; for whatever IS not from faith is sin.

I would interpret that Paul was challenging Peter that the Gentile believers were offended that they were not considered "good enough" to eat with and that was his argument. There is sensitivity to where other believers are in their journey of faith. A big controversy in some circles currently is whether a Christian should drink alcohol. We have the liberty to drink or eat anything (specifically though not to drunkenness), but we should not offend or cause someone to stumble as a result of our liberty. So there does need to be this kind of sensitivity in the church.

Paul's argument was about what happened at the church at Antioch. This was the first place believers were called Christians. This Gentile church had a broad cultural mix of people. People came from many different countries. This was Paul's home church for a while and I am sure that this great mix of people was discouraged that they might have been second class citizens in the church of Jesus Christ. So Paul thought it necessary to openly confront the issue.

What was Peter's reaction to this confrontation? Paul does not say but Peter references Paul in his last book and his last chapter:

2 Peter 3:15, 16 *and consider THAT the longsuffering of our Lord IS salvation—as also our beloved brother Paul, according to the wisdom given to him, has written to you, as also in all his epistles, speaking in them of these things, in which are some things hard to understand, which untaught and unstable PEOPLE twist to their own destruction, as THEY DO also the rest of the Scriptures.*

Peter loved Paul and appreciated his wisdom. And he went on to say that some of the things Paul wrote about were difficult to understand for the unlearned and unstable. It is interesting to note that Peter himself had been classified as "unlearned" by the Jewish leaders in court. But Peter was a stable man of God seeking Him with all his heart and he was used by God to get the church up and running playing a key leadership role. As a great general once said to his portrait artist, "paint me warts and all!" Peter was not perfect as none of us are, but Peter was willing, able, and did it!

There is a level of personal liberty in our faith in Jesus Christ. When we are in someone's home or we are their guests at some other venue we should have a heart to eat or drink whatever they put in front of us. If you were at my home and turned down my pork dinner it would actually be a judgment by you of my eating decisions and we are told to not judge others in these matters. So even though you might not eat pork in your own home you should understand you can eat that in my home if that is what I offer you as my guest.

The key to understand here is that each of us are allowed to eat whatever we have faith to eat. This means that if I believe I have freedom in Christ to eat my pork dinner then that pork dinner can be eaten by me for God has called it clean. If that pork stirs a question mark in my heart – where I wasn't sure whether it was proper for me or not to eat such a food – then I should not eat it on my own. Again even if I did not eat it by my choice I still should eat it as your guest.

We have walked with Peter throughout the Book of Acts. We have seen his boldness in action and the Power of God be released every step of the way. He above all others was the key figure to the birth of the church of Jesus Christ. He got the church up and running without an organization chart and without a five year plan given by Jesus Christ. He lived day by day tuned into the direction and leading of the Holy Spirit.

After Peter got everything started Jesus used the Apostle Paul to organize the church with doctrine and definitions for the clear truths to be found in the New Covenant and their differences with the Old Covenant. For example, the first deacons were chosen because they were men of good report and full of the Holy Spirit. Twenty years later Paul determined that these two requirements were not enough. So he set forth a list of requirements (1 Tim 3:8-13) that are to apply today to the qualifications of deacons (which hardly a church in America today even uses).

Let us consider the Power displayed by Peter in the book of Acts

- preached the first sermon
- saved the first converts
- healed the first sick person
- argued in court
- baptized in the Spirit new believers
- led the first Gentiles to the Lord
- he led the paradigm change to accept Gentiles into the New Covenant
- his shadow healed the sick
- raised the dead to life

He led a remarkable life for an unlearned fisherman who became a great fisher of man as he "fed the sheep of Jesus Christ."

The evidence is in and we discover that Peter found the Power that is available to every believer everywhere.

DISCUSSION CHAPTER FOURTEEN
PETER IN THE EPISTLES OF PAUL

1) What kinds of conflicted issues do you deal with as a Christian or some that maybe you grew up with in church?

2) Why did Paul not take Peter aside and handle the matter person to person?

3) How do we handle Christians from other denominations or groups different from our own?

4) Is it always wrong to be sensitive to the practices of other Christians?

5) What are some of the limitations we have put on ourselves in matters of where we go and what we do and eat?

Made in the USA
Charleston, SC
28 April 2012